the
Tillamook® Cheese
cookbook

the Tillamook® Cheese cookbook

CELEBRATING 100 YEARS *of* EXCELLENCE

Arnica Publishing, Inc.
Portland, Oregon

Library of Congress Cataloging-in-Publication Data

Holstad, Kathy, 1961-
  The Tillamook cheese cookbook : celebrating 100 years of excellence / [compiled by Kathy Holstad].
    p. cm.
  ISBN 978-0-9801942-4-1
  1. Cookery (Cheese) 2. Cheese--Oregon--Tillamook County. I. Tillamook County Creamery Association. II. Title.

TX759.5.C48H65 2009
641.3'73--dc22

             2008026856

Photos on pages xviii, 1, 6, 38, 40, 41, 58, 68, 69, 92, 94, 104, 130, 144, 148, 152, 154, 156, 158, 166, 170, 172, 174, 175, 176, 180
© Arnica Publishing, Inc.

Photos on pages 2, 10, 14, 18, 22, 26, 30, 34, 42, 46, 50, 54, 62, 66, 70, 74, 78, 82, 86, 90, 96, 100, 108, 112, 116, 120, 124, 128, 132, 136, 140, 162, 182
© Polara Studios

See page 193 for photography credits.
Images not acknowledged are copyright © Tillamook County Creamery Association, all rights reserved. Reprinted with permission.
Cover and text design: Aimee Genter and Emily García

Editorial Team:

Gloria Martinez, *editor-in-chief*
Rick Schafer, *creative director*
Dick Owsiany, *senior director of project development*
Aimee Genter, *senior graphic designer*
Emily García, *junior graphic designer*

Jennie Chamberlin, *copy editor*
Georgia Hill, *editorial assistant*
Mattie Ivy, *editorial assistant*
Michael Palodichuk, *editorial assistant*
Shannon Hunt, *editorial assistant*

Arnica Publishing, Inc.
3880 SE Eighth Ave, Suite 110
Portland, Oregon 97202
Phone: (503) 225-9900
Fax: (503) 225-9901
www.arnicacreative.com

NOTICE: Consumption of raw meats and seafood may increase your risk of contracting food-borne illnesses.

Arnica books are available at special discounts when purchased in bulk for premiums and sales promotions, as well as for fund-raising or educational use. Special editions or book excerption can also be created for specification. For details, contact the Sales Director at the address above.

*To the past and present farmer owners and the employees of the Tillamook County Creamery Association
who have worked diligently for 100 years to make Tillamook Cheese the best tasting, highest-quality cheese you can buy.
Their commitment to quality, consistency and taste is second to none...*

Tillamook tastes better because it's made better.

Table of Contents

Sandwiches & Pizza

Mac & Cheese

Main Course

Breakfast & Brunch

Desserts

Back Matter

P

In celebration of our 100th A

collection of our recipes but a glimpse into our rich h
hundreds of wonderful recipes ranging from super-si
mouth-watering desserts.

We view cheese making as an art form, and for us, th
farmers. At the heart of this recipe is fresh milk deliv
Tillamook cheese its characteristic creaminess and, a
recognized and enjoyed by cheese connoisseurs worl

Tillamook cheese and dairy farming are a part of my
Ezra Galloway, was a second generation Tillamook d
daughters, Judy and her husband Virgil took over the
retired. They farmed until the 1980s. As I grew up I
farm feeding the calves, collecting the eggs from the h
cows from the pastures to the milking parlor. After th
whole family would meet at the breakfast table for A
pancakes. Uncle Virgil would bring a bucket of fresh
parlor, the cream still settled on top.

Because of my heritage, I have a great amount of res]
dairy farmers—it is not an easy occupation. It is a tw
seven-day-a-week job to care for your animals and y
farmer requires expertise in business, nutrition, anin
among many other talents. Our dairy farmers, as we
pride in our history. They work diligently to maintai
and consistently produce premium-quality cheese. V
and experience can be tasted in every bite.

Dairy products, especially cheese, are such an integr;
amazingly diverse and delicious food—you can melt
Our Tillamook Cheese Cookbook is full of the recij
share them with you! Enjoy!

Foreword

As the head cheesemaker for the Tillamook County Creamery Association, it is my duty to ensure that every batch of Tillamook Cheese meets our high standards of quality, consistency, and taste. Nearly 100 years of cheese-making experience goes into making our award-winning Cheddar.

Harley Christensen, on the right, and another cheesemaker pile curd by hand in an open vat at one of the little creameries. Circa mid-1940s.

Cheese making is a skill that I learned by doing. As one of four children of dairy-farming parents in Hebo during the early 1950s, I used to get up at the crack of dawn every morning to milk our family's twenty-eight cows before heading off to school. My father was the cheesemaker at the Hebo Cheese Plant, and my mother took care of the daily chores on our dairy farm.

When I was seventeen, I began learning the art of cheese making. Each baby loaf was made individually at the time, and every detail of the process was performed by hand.

It wasn't long after that all of the small cheese plants in Tillamook County were consolidated and milk was brought to the current Tillamook Creamery to be made into cheese. We used to make the forty-pound blocks of cheese, and wrap them in waxed paper—just like Christmas presents—then we melted the wax to seal around the product and preserve freshness. At that time, I was so skinny I didn't even weigh enough to pull the rope to dip the forty-pounders! This was very hard work, but I loved it.

Over the years, I've seen a lot change—but one thing has never changed and that is the dedication of our farmers, our employees and our cheesemakers to make the highest-quality, best-tasting cheese possible. Of that, I am very proud.

—Dale Baumgartner

The Tillamook Tradition

In Tillamook County on the Oregon Coast, known for its pristine beauty with green valleys and stunning coast line, you may notice that cows outnumber people. Over the years moderate climate and plentiful rain have made this area ideal for dairy farming. Today the Tillamook County Creamery Association (TCCA), known as the makers of famous Tillamook cheese, consists of 120 family dairy farms that ship their milk daily to the creamery to be made into cheese and ice cream. In celebration of our 100th Anniversary we wanted to share our rich history with you as well as our wonderful recipes. This is how it all began…

In 1909, ten small independent cheese plants in Tillamook County joined together to form the Tillamook County Creamery Association. The co-op grew out of the desire of a handful of farmers to ensure that the cheese produced in the area was of the absolute highest quality. After all, these were the dedicated people who actually worked the soil and milked the cows. They wanted the products made from their milk to reflect their care and commitment. They also wanted to build a community and pass the farms and the dairy-farm lifestyle down to the generations to come. Profits from the cooperative have been shared to sustain family farms since the beginning and this has sustained the Tillamook Tradition for a century.

The story behind this award-winning cheese actually began back in 1854, when several dairy farmers banded together to construct a two-masted schooner, dubbed the *Morning Star of Tillamook*, to transport their butter to Portland, Oregon. An image of the *Morning Star* is proudly displayed on the Tillamook label to this day.

In 1894, T.S. Townsend, a successful dairy industry entrepreneur, established the first commercial cheese plant in Tillamook. Townsend hired Peter McIntosh, a Canadian cheesemaker experienced with the Cheddaring process. McIntosh brought a recipe for Cheddar cheese with him and his influence and skill soon earned him the title "Cheese King of the Coast." In fact, he was so fine a cheesemaker that they still use his recipe to this day.

It was not long before the local talented cheesemakers were recognized outside Oregon for their abilities. A cheese from Tillamook county won its first award in 1904 at the St. Louis World's Fair. These early accolades helped our cheesemakers establish a reputation beyond the county and consistently earned them top honors in dairy product contests.

In the late 1940s, four of the larger independent plants merged and a centrally located creamery was built just north of the town of Tillamook where it remains today.

Over the last century the Tillamook Creamery and the farmer-owners have remained committed to the core values of quality, consistency and great taste that their consumers have come to expect. To accomplish this they use the highest-quality, freshest milk that arrives daily to make Tillamook Cheese. All of the milk comes from cows that have not been treated with the artificial growth hormone, Rbst. The all-natural Cheddar is made slowly and aged with time in order to develop that perfect flavor and texture for which Tillamook Cheese is prized.

TCCA remains committed to carrying on the traditions that were established by the founding fathers of the cooperative so many years ago. As it was 100 years ago, and as it remains today, Tillamook Cheese tastes better because it's made better!

1855: *Morning Star II* on the Tillamook Bay in the summer of 1959, setting sail for Oregon's Centennial Celebration in Portland. The original *Morning Star of Tillamook* (aka *Morning Star*) was built in late 1854 and launched by settlers on Jan. 5, 1855, to transport their goods, which included butter, to outside markets. The *Morning Star* was the first ship built and registered in the Oregon Territory. In November 1860, the *Morning Star* was lost in the Straight of Juan de Fuca. This replica of the original schooner was built in celebration of the Oregon centennial and sailed with a six-ton cargo of Tillamook cheese, stopping at different ports to deliver the cheese to customers. Years later, the schooner was placed on the front lawn of the Tillamook Cheese plant.

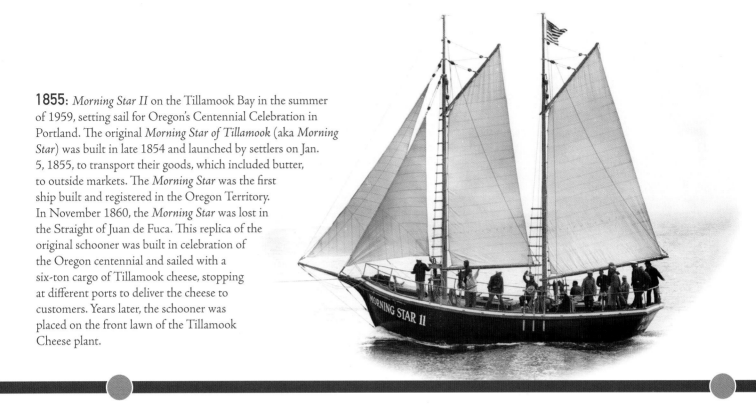

1885: The family and friends of Warren N. and Harriet Trask Vaughn on the Vaughn's farm.

1900: Two Tillamook pioneer dairy farmers on an ox-drawn cart.

1910: The Tillamook Creamery, circa 1910. Jesse Earl, a farmer, sits in the wagon with the white horse, near the building. The dairy farmers would deliver their milk to the creamery closest to their farm in a horse and wagon. Creameries were the social center for each community. For many, it was the only opportunity to chat with people other than their family.

1922: Bessie Barber and her younger brother, Rip, stand next to a 350 to 450 pound cheese press in the Holstein creamery.

1926: Wanda Woodward of NBC sorts through fan mail. Photo used in an ad for a Tillamook recipe contest.

How the contest recipes come in - and booklet requests, too !

1931: The Little Holland Orchestra, which was a part of the Little Holland Program. The program aired on the Pacific Coast Network.

1945: A truck is backed up to a creamery picking up a load of cheese.

1949: At the Western Condensery in 1949. Tom Kehoe (atop the truck) fills the tanker truck with condensed whey.

1952: A display of Tillamook's award-winning cheddars. The trophy was the highest score trophy awarded to Albert Headinger, a Tillamook cheesemaker, in 1952 at the National Cheese Scoring Contest held in Waterloo, Iowa.

1956: A display and contest, "Guess mama's weight and get baby free!" in Don's Market in 1956.

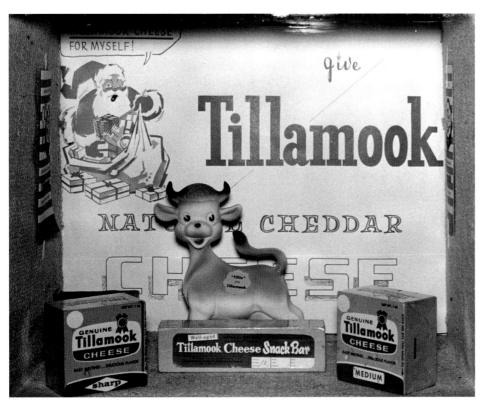

1958: Tillie of Tillamook, the squeaky toy, in a Christmas display promoting Tillamook cheese. Circa 1958. Tillie was used in a variety of advertisements and displays during the 1950s and 1960s. Her first appearance was of a cartoon cow in Tillamook Cheese print ads. The original squeaky toy came about in 1958, a replica of Tillie has been made for the 100th Anniversary celebration of Tillamook Cheese.

1958: Miss USA Charlotte Sheffield visited ten Portland-area Safeway stores to promote Safeway and Tillamook Cheese, March 19–21, 1958. Here she is making an appearance at one of the Safeway stores in Portland.

1958: Margaret Mailer, who often conducted Tillamook cheese demonstrations, conducts a demo in the Pantry Market in Pasadena, Calif.

1959: Jack LaLanne, famous bodybuilder and future exercise guru, promotes Tillamook cheese in a publicity shot.

1963: Tillamook cheese as a Cracker Barrel Feature.

1963: The Oregon Dairy Princess promotes Tillamook cheese at a local Fred Meyer store.

They're raising the bounty of Tillamook County.

Every cheese lover west of the Rockies knows the reputation of Tillamook, one of the world's leading natural cheddars. It's so good that, until recently, production couldn't keep up with demand.

That's when Beale Dixon, General Manager, and Spencer George, Production Manager of Tillamook County Creamery Association, took a crucial first step for the cheese industry. They installed in their packaging department a new highly sophisticated Cryovac® system for wrapping their delicious cheddar in our transparent laminated film, with a production capacity of up to 160 consumer packages per minute.

Now there's a bountiful supply of Tillamook cheese to satisfy the steadily increasing market demand.

Tillamook's success is another example of what happens when the changers in a company meet with Cryovac to challenge "status quo" thinking. Maybe our innovative ideas in custom laminate packaging and processing can help you, too, achieve new status in the market.

Cryovac Division,
W.R. Grace & Co.,
Duncan, South Carolina 29334,
and Mississauga, Ontario L4Y 2A2. **CRYOVAC**

Beale Dixon, General Manager (right),
Spencer George, Production Manager
Tillamook County Creamery Association
Tillamook, Oregon

1970s: Beale Dixon, TCCA general manager, and Spencer George, TCCA production manager, promote Cryovac, a new system that was installed in the packaging department. Circa early 1970s.

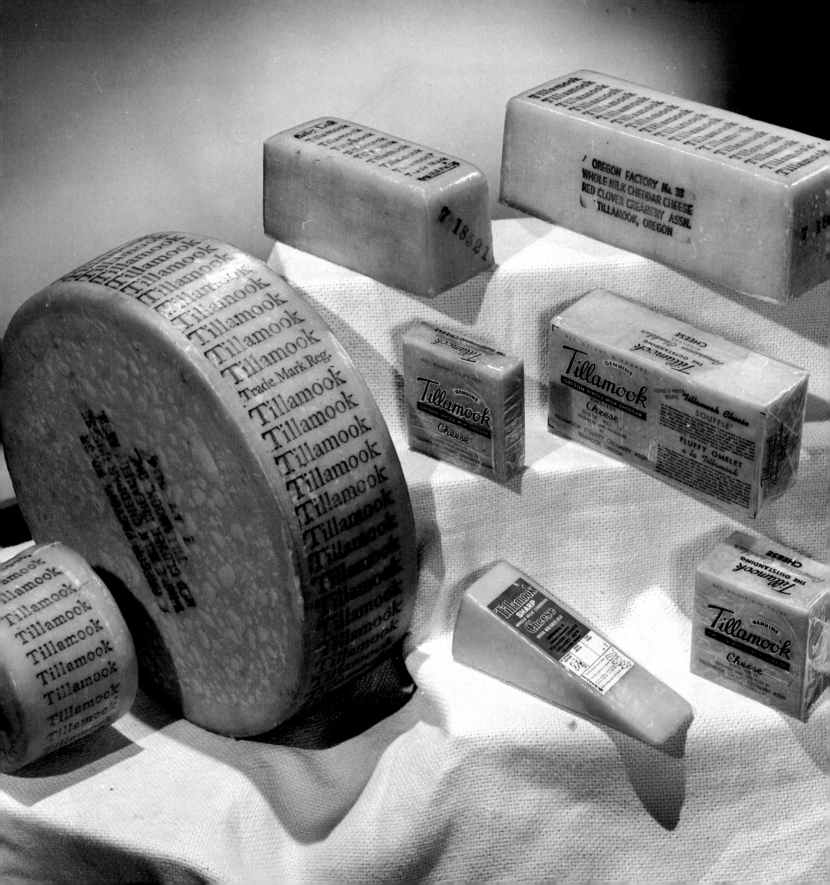

How to Make Cheese:
Homemade White Cheddar

The recipe yields about 2.6 pounds of cheese per batch, though it will take a little time (4 hours cooking, 5 hours drying, and 100 days of aging) before you can taste the fruits of your labor. If you can't wait that long, just go to the store and pick up a Baby Loaf of Tillamook Vintage White Medium Cheddar Cheese.

INGREDIENTS

1/2 Junket rennet tablet (solidifying enzyme)
3 gallons of (3.2%) pasteurized homogenized whole milk
1 pint (2 cups) half & half cream
1 1/2 cups buttermilk (as fresh as possible)
1 ounce (5 teaspoons) salt
1/4 cup cold water

EQUIPMENT

Large cookie sheet
Cooking pot large enough to hold 3 gallons of milk
Sharp knife long enough to cut depth of cooking pot
Electric range
Instant-read thermometer with a range from 80°F to 120°F
Large wooden spoon or spatula
Large colander (at least 11 inches in diameter)
Cheesecloth: 20 by 20-inch square
Heavy skillet or other 4 to 5-pound weight for pressing cheese

PREPARATION

1. Crush and dissolve half the Junket rennet tablet in 1/4 cup of cold water. Set aside. Allow the tablet to dissolve for two hours.

2. Place the pot on the burner, and add the milk and cream. The cream will bring the mixture to the desired 4.2 percent milkfat.

3. Heat the milk mixture to 88°F, but quickly remove the pot if the milk exceeds 88°F.

4. Add the buttermilk (culture), and stir it into the heated milk.

5. Let the mixture sit and "ripen" at 88°F for 45 minutes. This activates the culture. (The culture produces lactic acid to break up the amino acids in the milk, which brings about the flavor of the cheese.)

6. Remove the cooking pot from the heat and add the dissolved Junket rennet tablet-water mixture to the milk. Stir rapidly in one direction with a large wooden spoon and then back-stir for 30 seconds. The Junket rennet will cause the milk to "set," or thicken into a gelatin-like consistency.

7. Record the time (called the "set" time) at which the Junket rennet was added. You will need it as a reference point for steps 12 and 14. Let the milk "set" for 30 minutes without stirring. This will make the "curd."

8. Using a long knife, cut the curd into a crisscross pattern 3/8-inch square.

9. Allow the curd to sit and "heal" for 10 minutes without stirring.

10. Place the cooking pot back over a low heat and during the next 40 minutes, slowly raise the temperature to 100°F while stirring. Increase the temperature about 1 degree every 3 minutes, adjusting the heat if needed. When it reaches 100°F, remove the pot from the heat.

11. Stir gently and regularly for another 40 minutes as the mixture separates into solid curd and liquid whey.

12. It should now be 2 hours since the rennet was added. (Refer to your recorded time in step 7). Pour the curds into the colander, allowing the liquid whey to drain off for 10 minutes.

13. Place the mass of drained curd on a cookie sheet to "knit" together, or congeal. Using a spatula, turn the mass of curd over every 30 minutes for the next 2 hours. As you do so, the curd continues to knit. Wipe away the whey that drains off.

Clockwise from top left:

Pete Hoffert, on the left, and another cheesemaker cut the curds so they can expel the whey.

Cheesemaker Frank Hittick flips the curd during the cheesemaking process.

Cheese curds are pressed into the ring molds. Molds were lined with cheese cloth and filled by hand and then pressed to expel the whey. It was a very physically active process of cranking the press tighter and tighter to expel the whey.

The cheese ripening room, where shelf, after shelf, after shelf of Tillamook cheese would rest and ripen until being shipped to a customer.

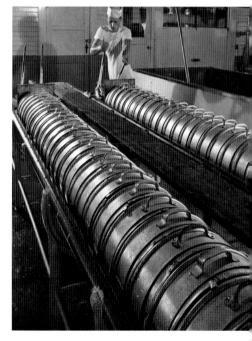

14. When it has been 3 1/2 hours since the rennet was added, (refer, again, to the recorded time in step 7), slice the mass of curd into 1/2-inch cubes.

15. Using your hands, gently stir the salt into the curd. This slows the natural production of acid. (Salt also expels moisture and adds flavor.)

16. Clean the colander and line it with the cheesecloth. Then pour in the curds. Form a pouch from the cheesecloth by gathering together the 4 corners and tying them into a knot. (Or, wrap it with a rubber band or a piece of string.) Squeeze the pouch of curd until no more liquid whey drains from it.

17. Set the pouch in a location where it can continue to drain slowly for 4 or 5 hours under the pressure of a 4 to 5 pound weight. A heavy skillet or a sturdy saucepan filled half full with water works well as a cheese press. Do not put the cheese in a closed container, as air circulation is important. After the cheese has been pressed, hang it to dry for 24 hours at room temperature.

18. Remove the cheesecloth. Seal the bare cheese in aluminum foil and resealable plastic bags. Wrap the cheese tightly and use a straw or household syringe to remove as much air as possible from the bag. Place this inside another plastic bag for added protection against unwanted bacteria. For best results, use a vacuum sealer if you have one available.

19. With a permanent marker, write today's date on the plastic bag. Refrigerate the cheese, unopened, for 100 days. Be patient—opening the package lets in new bacteria. When your cheese is finished aging, open the package and cut off any bacteria that may have formed.

Now, enjoy your homemade White Cheddar cheese!

CHEF'S NOTE
Junket rennet is available in your supermarket in the pudding section.

TOP (l to r):
Michael, Joyce,
Jessica, April

BOTTOM (l to r):
Angela, Chuck,
Esther

Appetizers

Chuck and Esther Bailey
Bailey Farms Inc.

*"We work hard to be successful and we care about the land,
the animals, and the products we produce."*

In the late 1890s, the Bailey family made the arduous trek from Tennessee to the Willamette Valley. By 1895, David Bailey had established a dairy near Cloverdale. In the evenings, after milking the cows by hand, the cans of milk were cooled by setting them in cold water until it was time to transport them to the creamery by horse and wagon the next day.

Today, the Bailey family still maintains a large farm, 100 acres of which are from the original property. Chuck, grandson of David, says he enjoys the independent lifestyle that comes with being a dairy farmer, and the "challenge to be successful and develop our dairy into a business that is successful and supports multiple generations of our family is what motivates me daily." It is hard work, but the goal is always to produce the highest-quality milk.

Cheese Truffles

These rich and creamy truffles will melt in your mouth.

Makes approximately 24 truffles

INGREDIENTS
2 teaspoons olive oil
2 tablespoons minced shallots
Pinch of salt
1 cup (4 ounces) Tillamook Monterey
  Jack cheese, broken into chunks
1 cup (4 ounces) Tillamook Vintage
  White Extra Sharp Cheddar cheese,
  broken into chunks
2 1/2 tablespoons Tillamook unsalted
  butter
1 1/2 teaspoons brandy or cognac
1 tablespoon finely minced celery
Pinch of cayenne
1/4 cup fine dried bread crumbs
1 tablespoon freshly minced parsley

PREPARATION
Heat the oil in a small frying pan over medium heat. Add the shallots and season with salt. Sauté until the shallots are tender. Set aside to cool.

Place the cheeses, butter, and brandy in a food processor. Pulse until the mixture is smooth.

Transfer the cheese mixture to a medium bowl and stir in the shallots, celery, and cayenne. Chill in the refrigerator for 1/2 hour. Combine the bread crumbs and parsley in a separate bowl.

Form the chilled cheese mixture into teaspoon-sized balls. Roll the cheese balls in the bread crumb mixture. Serve at room temperature.

CHEF'S NOTE
These truffles can be made a few days in advance and refrigerated. Bring to room temperature before serving. The cheese mixture can also be made into a log or a large ball, and served with crackers.

Aged Cheddar
with Apple Wedges and Cider Reduction

Cheddar and apples—with the tartness of cider.

Makes 8 servings

INGREDIENTS
2 Granny Smith apples, cored
2 cups apple cider
2 teaspoons Tillamook butter, chilled
8 slices walnut or other nut bread, toasted, halved
1/2 pound Tillamook Aged Cheddar cheese, thinly sliced
1 cup roasted pecans

PREPARATION
Cut each apple into 16 slices. Bring the cider to a boil in a large saucepan. Cook until it has reduced to 1/2 cup, about 15 minutes. Remove from the heat. Add the butter, and stir with a whisk until the butter melts.

Place 2 bread halves on each of 8 dessert plates. Divide the cheese slices evenly among the bread halves. Place 2 apple slices on each bread half. Drizzle 1 tablespoon of cider reduction around each serving. Garnish with roasted pecans.

Aged Cheese Facts

As Cheddar cheese ages, it becomes sharper, harder, and more crumbly. An aged cheese that crumbles when sliced represents a cheese that has aged exceptionally well, so slice and enjoy!

Tillamook cheese is naturally aged, which means it is common to develop a small amount of moisture inside the package. In our longer-aged cheeses, the proteins in the cheese will give up moisture during the aging process. You may simply wipe off the excess moisture and enjoy.

Baked Mini Cheese Puffs
with Chives

This light appetizer is a perfect balance of cheddar and chives.

Makes 2 dozen puffs

INGREDIENTS
2 tablespoons Tillamook butter
3/4 cup all-purpose flour
1/2 teaspoon salt
1/2 cup Tillamook Finely Shredded
    Medium Cheddar cheese
2 tablespoons chopped chives
2 large eggs
3/4 cup whole milk
1/4 cup water

PREPARATION
Preheat the oven to 375°F.

Butter the cups of a 24-cup, non-stick mini-muffin pan. Mix together the flour, salt, cheese and chives in small bowl. Using a bowl with a pour spout, whisk together the eggs, milk and water. Add the flour mixture, and whisk until the ingredients are blended, but still lumpy. Heat the muffin pan in the oven for 2 minutes. Remove, and divide the batter evenly among the muffin cups.

Bake for 20 minutes until the puffs are golden. Quickly cut a small slit in each puff for the steam to escape. Serve immediately.

Tillamook Cheese Nachos

Simple, but just the right south-of-the-border flavor.

Serves 6 to 8

INGREDIENTS
1 pound corn tortilla chips
2 cups refried beans
1 (8-ounce) package (2 cups) shredded Tillamook Pepper Jack cheese
1 (8-ounce) package (2 cups) shredded Tillamook Medium Cheddar cheese

GARNISH
1/2 cup chopped olives
3/4 cup purchased salsa
1/2 cup chopped green onions
1/3 cup Tillamook sour cream
1/3 cup purchased guacamole

PREPARATION
Arrange the chips and beans and top with the cheeses in a shallow baking dish. Microwave until the cheese melts. Garnish with the olives, salsa, onions, sour cream, and guacamole. Serve immediately.

Fresh Salsa

"This is a nice appetizer to serve in the summertime—a little more than just salsa and every time I serve it people beg for the recipe!" —Deborah Luther

Serves 6 to 8

INGREDIENTS
6 ripe tomatoes, finely chopped
1 white onion, finely chopped
1 bunch green onions, chopped
1 bunch cilantro, chopped
2 cloves garlic, minced or pressed
1 large jalapeño (or more to taste), finely chopped
1 ripe avocado, finely chopped
1 to 2 tablespoons freshly squeezed lime or lemon juice
1 can sliced black olives
1 (8-ounce) package (2 cups) shredded Medium Tillamook Cheddar cheese
1 (8-ounce) package (2 cups) shredded Tillamook Monterey Jack cheese
Salt
Freshly ground black pepper

PREPARATION
Stir all the ingredients together. Season to taste with salt and pepper. Serve with fresh tortilla chips or on top of nachos. (This salsa is also a perfect addition to ground beef served in a taco salad.)

Submitted by Deborah Luther
Tillamook Cheese Recipe Contest 2001
La Habra, CA

Fondue au Fromage

These days, when cheese gets old or dries out it is usually thrown away. The same system applies to stale bread; it is either tossed away or fed to the birds. It was not always done this way. Thanks to Swiss farmers back in the eighteenth century, we now enjoy a wonderful dish called fondue au fromage (cheese fondue) and its many variations. Farmers in the Swiss Alps were isolated from larger towns during the freezing winter months and therefore had to sustain their food supplies for much longer than city dwellers. When their cheese and bread became stale and unappetizing, the farmers experimented and soon realized that the cheese tasted much better when it was melted. As they dipped the stale bread into the warmed cheese, it softened and became much more tasty as well. Eventually people started to mix milk and/or wine into the melted cheese and, voilà—a more modern version of fondue was born!

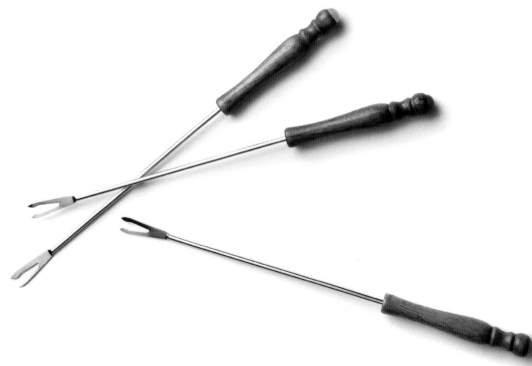

French Fondue Tillamook-Style

Serves 4 to 6

INGREDIENTS
1 clove garlic
2 tablespoons Tillamook butter
3 tablespoons chopped chives
1 cup very dry white wine
4 cups shredded Tillamook Sharp
  Cheddar cheese
3 tablespoons all-purpose flour
Freshly ground black pepper
1/8 teaspoon nutmeg
Salt

PREPARATION
Rub the top of the container of a double boiler or chafing dish with the clove of garlic. Add the butter, chives, and wine. Heat to the boiling point. Add the cheese and flour slowly, stirring in one direction until the cheese melts.

Add the pepper, nutmeg, and salt while stirring. Keep the fondue warm over a chafing dish or feed warmer.

Cheese Fondue

Serves 4 to 6

INGREDIENTS
1 clove garlic, crushed
1 1/4 cups dry white wine
Pinch of nutmeg
Pinch of freshly ground black pepper
Pinch of garlic powder
1 1/2 cups Tillamook Sharp Cheddar
  cheese
1 1/2 cups Tillamook Monterey Jack
  cheese
2 teaspoons cornstarch dissolved in 1/4
  cup dry, white wine
1 ounce sherry
1 loaf French bread, cubed

PREPARATION
Rub a shallow, wide fondue dish with the garlic. Add the wine, nutmeg, pepper, and garlic powder. Bring the mixture to simmer over medium heat.

Combine the cheese, and add to the wine mixture in 4 batches, constantly stirring until smooth. Gradually stir in the cornstarch mixture (do not boil.) Stir in the sherry, and serve over a warmer with skewers. Allow the diners to skewer the bread cubes and dip into the fondue dish.

Created by Marcel Lasheme,
Executive Regional Chef
Jake's Famous Crawfish Restaurant
Portland, Oregon

Cheddar & Beer Fondue

Makes 3 cups
Serves 8 as an appetizer

INGREDIENTS

1 pound new potatoes
4 links (about 1 pound) fresh Bratwurst
  or other mild pork sausage
1 1/2 cups shredded Tillamook
  Monterey Jack cheese
1 1/2 cups shredded Tillamook Vintage
  White Medium Cheddar cheese
1 1/2 cups shredded Tillamook Vintage
  White Extra Sharp Cheddar cheese
1 tablespoon all-purpose flour
1 1/2 teaspoons dry mustard
1 cup amber ale, chilled
1 1/2 teaspoons Worcestershire sauce
1/2 teaspoon Tabasco® pepper sauce
3 cups multigrain bread, cubed to
  1-inch

PREPARATION

Preheat the oven to 375°F.

Wash and quarter the potatoes. Boil them in salted water until they are fork-tender.

Cut the sausage links diagonally into thick slices. Bake on a foil-lined cookie sheet for about 15 minutes until cooked.

Toss the cheeses with the flour and mustard in a medium bowl. Whisk the ale with Worcestershire and pepper sauce in a 2-quart saucepan set over medium heat. Add the cheese, whisking constantly until the cheese has melted and the mixture is smooth. Bring to a simmer and continue to stir until the fondue thickens. Pour immediately into a heated fondue pot. Serve with the prepared bread, potatoes, and sausage.

Crunchy Cornsticks
with Chilis & Cheddar

A traditional snack with a little something extra.

Makes 28 cornsticks

INGREDIENTS
Melted shortening or bacon fat for the molds
1 cup yellow cornmeal
1 cup, plus 2 tablespoons unbleached all-purpose flour
2 teaspoons baking powder
1 teaspoon baking soda
2 teaspoons cumin
1 teaspoon high-quality chili powder
1 teaspoon salt
1 (17-ounce) can creamed corn
1 cup buttermilk
4 tablespoons (1/2 stick) Tillamook unsalted butter, melted
2 large eggs
1 1/4 cups grated Tillamook Sharp Cheddar cheese
1 can (4-ounces) minced green chilis

SPECIAL EQUIPMENT
Cornstick molds

PREPARATION
Preheat the oven to 350°F. Lightly coat the cornstick molds with the melted shortening or bacon fat.

Stir the cornmeal, flour, baking powder, baking soda, cumin, chili powder, and salt together in a medium mixing bowl.

Whisk the creamed corn, buttermilk, butter, and eggs together in a large mixing bowl. Add the cornmeal mixture to the corn mixture and stir just until combined. Add the Cheddar and chilis, and fold just until they are evenly distributed.

Spoon the batter into the prepared molds, filling each two-thirds full. Bake until the cornsticks are crusty and golden-brown, about 10 to 12 minutes.

Allow to cool slightly, then turn out onto a wire rack to cool completely. If necessary, repeat with the remaining batter, lightly coating the molds with melted fat after each batch.

Submitted by Cathy Davis,
KSJN Radio Recipe Contest

Puff Pastry Straws

"This simple and tasty recipe can fill your house with great whiffs of freshly baked pastry just as guests are arriving. Now, with good-quality packaged puff pastry available, you can accomplish in minutes what used to take hours in our kitchen when we made everything from scratch." —Chef Ron Paul, Portland, Oregon

Makes 5 1/2 dozen crisps

INGREDIENTS
3 pounds puff pastry
6 cups grated Tillamook Sharp Cheddar
 cheese
Pinch of cayenne pepper

PREPARATION
Preheat the oven to 350°F.

Roll out the puff pastry to 1/4-inch thickness and allow to rest. Sprinkle the cheese on half of the puff pastry. Sprinkle with the cayenne pepper. Fold over the other half of the puff pastry and press lightly. Cut into 1/2-inch thick strips. Place on a cookie sheet covered with parchment paper.

Bake for 10 to 15 minutes, and serve immediately.

RIGHT: The state inspector examining a milk shipment in milk receiving at the new, centrally located Tillamook cheese plant, circa 1952. The milk receiving area is where the milk was first inspected and samples would be taken to test for quality. Full milk cans were delivered by the farmers to the milk receiving area where they were unloaded onto the milk chain, which was an automatic, continuous belt conveyor that ran the cans into the receiving room. There the cans were emptied, washed and sent back out to the waiting farmers.

Cheddar Crisps

A delightful snack or appetizer for entertaining.

Makes 5 1/2 dozen crisps

INGREDIENTS

1/2 cup (1 stick) Tillamook butter, cut into 6 pieces
1/4 cup rice flour
3/4 cup all-purpose flour
1 cup shredded Special Reserve Extra Sharp Tillamook Cheddar cheese
3/4 teaspoon Tabasco® pepper sauce
1 teaspoon Worcestershire sauce
1/4 teaspoon salt
1/4 teaspoon finely chopped fresh rosemary
1/4 teaspoon coarsely ground black pepper

SPECIAL EQUIPMENT
Parchment paper

PREPARATION

Place the butter, flours, cheese, pepper sauce, Worcestershire and salt in the bowl of a food processor. Process for about one minute or until the mixture begins to form a smooth ball. Remove the dough from the bowl and divide it into thirds.

Quickly knead each portion, adding the rosemary to one, black pepper to another, and leaving the last portion plain. Form each portion into a 4-inch log.

Wrap each log with plastic wrap and chill until firm, or overnight.

Preheat the oven to 400ºF. Cut the chilled logs into thin slices (approx 22 per roll) and place 1 inch apart on parchment-lined baking sheets. Bake 8 to 9 minutes, or until lightly browned. Allow the crisps to cool on the baking sheet for 3 minutes before transferring them to a wire rack to finish cooling.

Potato Cheddar Rounds

Simple and delicious!

Makes 28 to 30 appetizers

INGREDIENTS
2 cups mashed potatoes, chilled
1/2 cup grated Tillamook Medium
  Cheddar cheese
1 egg
1 tablespoon milk
1/2 cup dry bread crumbs

PREPARATION
Preheat the broiler.

Combine the potatoes and cheese in a medium bowl and blend well. Shape the mixture into 28 to 30 balls. In a separate bowl, whisk together the egg and milk. Dip the balls in the egg, then roll in bread crumbs.

Place the balls on a baking sheet. Broil, 5 inches from the heat, for 4 to 6 minutes, or until they are golden-brown. Turn, and brown the other side about 4 minutes. Serve warm on wooden toothpicks.

Italian Cheese Melts

A fresh and cheesy start to any meal.

Makes 16 to 20 pieces

INGREDIENTS

2 whole loaves Italian bread
   (approximately 1 pound each)
1/2 cup bottled balsamic vinaigrette
   dressing
1 (2-pound) package (about 8 cups)
   Tillamook Fancy Medium Cheddar
   Shredded cheese
2/3 cup coarsely chopped fresh basil
8 medium Roma tomatoes, thinly sliced
Salt
Freshly ground black pepper
1/2 cup sliced, pitted kalamata olives

PREPARATION

Preheat the oven to 400°F.

Cut the bread in half lengthwise. Place the halves, cut-sides-up, on a baking sheet.

Toast the bread in the oven for 10 minutes. Brush the cut sides of the bread with the vinaigrette.

Toss the cheese with the basil. Divide the cheese into 4 portions and cover evenly over each bread half. Arrange the tomatoes on top of the cheese. Season to taste with salt and pepper. Scatter the olives on top.

Bake until the cheese melts, about 10 minutes. Cut each bread half into 4 or 5 pieces to serve.

SERVING SUGGESTION

Cut into slices and serve with mixed fresh salad greens tossed with vinaigrette.

LEFT TO RIGHT:

"Tillamook's Key to the Cupboard" Circa 1950s

"54 Prize Winning Tillamook Full Cream Cheese Recipes" One of the recipe books that consumers would write away for, as complied by Genevieve Callahan, Sunset magazine editor. Circa 1933.

"Tillamook Baker's Dozen Idea Book" Circa 1940s.

"Prize Winning Tillamook Whole Milk Cheese Recipes" One of the recipe books that consumers could write away for. Circa 1934.

Grilled Baby Potatoes
Stuffed with Tillamook Sharp Cheddar Cheese & Pancetta

Elegant and delicious—a twist on twice-baked potatoes.

Serves 4 to 6 as an appetizer

INGREDIENTS

8 baby or fingerling potatoes (each measuring about 1 1/2 inches across)
1 tablespoon salt
2 ounces pancetta (Italian-style bacon), diced
2 teaspoons olive oil
2 cloves garlic, minced
1 teaspoon freshly minced rosemary
2 to 3 tablespoons milk
3/4 cup grated Tillamook Sharp Cheddar cheese
Salt
Freshly ground black pepper
2 teaspoons freshly minced chives

SPECIAL EQUIPMENT

Small-holed grill rack

PREPARATION

Place the potatoes in a medium saucepan with 4 cups of water. Add the salt and bring to boil over high heat. Reduce the heat to medium, and simmer for 10 to 15 minutes, or until potatoes are tender. Do not overcook or let the potato skins crack. Drain, and set aside to cool until lukewarm.

While the potatoes are cooking, sauté the pancetta in olive oil over medium-high heat until crisp. Remove with a slotted spoon and drain on a paper towel. Remove all but 2 teaspoons of fat from the pan. Add the garlic and sauté over medium heat until softened, being careful not to brown the garlic. Stir in the rosemary, and continue to cook about 2 minutes. Remove from the heat, and set aside.

Preheat the grill to medium heat.

Cut the potatoes in half, gently scoop out the centers, and place in a small bowl. Add 2 tablespoons of milk, and mash with a fork. Add more milk if needed to make a creamy consistency. Stir in the pancetta, garlic, rosemary, and cheese. Season to taste with salt and pepper. Stuff the cheese mixture evenly into the potato skins.

Place the stuffed potatoes on a small-holed grill rack and grill for approximately 8 minutes, or until the skins are crisp and the filling is warm.

Sprinkle with chives and serve.

Aram Cheese Slices

This recipe showcases a variety of flavors and textures.

Serves 8 to 10

INGREDIENTS

Butter, for spreading on bread

1 package of pre-moistened Lavosh Bread (Armenian cracker bread)

20 slices Tillamook Medium Cheddar cheese

1 1/2 cups finely chopped candied pecans

20 slices Tillamook Swiss cheese

1 pomegranate (for red seeds)

1 (8-ounce) package of cream cheese, softened

2 tablespoons Tillamook butter, softened

2 sprigs fresh dill, finely chopped

1/3 cup finely chopped celery

1/3 cup finely chopped green bell pepper

PREPARATION

Spread butter evenly on 3 sheets of Lavosh bread. On the first sheet, cover with a layer of Cheddar, then follow with a layer of pecans. Roll up.

On a second sheet, cover with a layer of Swiss, then a layer of pomegranate seeds. Roll up.

Blend the cream cheese and butter together. Fold in the dill, celery, and bell pepper. Spread the mixture evenly on a third sheet of Lavosh bread. Roll up. Wrap all three rolls individually in plastic wrap and refrigerate for 2 hours. Cut into 1-inch rounds, and serve.

How to seed a pomegranate

To peel a pomegranate, first cut off the crown and gently scoop out some of the center core without disturbing the seeds. With a sharp knife, score just through the outer rind around the fruit in quarters. Put your thumb in the core center and gently pull apart the sections. Peel away the inner white papery skin covering the seeds and discard. Gently invert the skin inside out. To separate the white membrane from the pips, place the cut pieces in a bowl of cold water and gently separate the juicy seeds. The membrane pieces should float to the top of the water for easy separation.

Tillamook Cheddar & Jalapeño Dip

A perfectly spicy way to add a little kick to any gathering!

Serves 6 to 8

INGREDIENTS
2 cups shredded Tillamook Pepper Jack cheese
2 cups shredded Tillamook Medium Cheddar cheese
2 cups sliced jalapeños
4 cups mayonnaise
1 red bell pepper, chopped
1 bunch green onions, chopped

PREPARATION
Blend the cheese and the mayonnaise until they are well blended. Add the remaining ingredients and chill overnight.

Serve with chips or crackers and enjoy!

Smoked Salmon Dip

An easy-to-make dip, with the delicious flavors of the Northwest.

Serves 8 to 10

INGREDIENTS
8 ounces smoked salmon, flaked
1/4 cup mayonnaise
1/4 cup cream cheese, softened
2 cups shredded Tillamook Vintage
  White Extra Sharp Cheddar cheese
1 tablespoon freshly chopped dill
Tortilla chips or crackers

PREPARATION
Preheat the oven to 400°F.

Crumble the salmon into small pieces in a mixing bowl (check for and discard any bones).

Add the mayonnaise, cream cheese, and the cheese. Mix well so that the flavors are blended together. Fold in the dill.

Spread the mixture evenly into an ovenproof dish, and bake for 10 minutes. Or, microwave until the mixture is hot to touch.

Serve with your choice of tortilla chips or crackers on the side.

Created by Billy Hahn, Executive Chef
Jake's Famous Crawfish Restaurant
Portland, Oregon

Herbed Tomato Cheese Toasts

A great way to enjoy summer tomatoes.

Makes 10 toasts

INGREDIENTS
10 (1-inch) slices Italian bread
5 cups shredded Tillamook Special
   Reserve Extra Sharp Cheddar cheese
10 slices plum tomato, or 5 slices ripe
   tomato, halved
Salt
Freshly ground black pepper
1/2 cup freshly minced thyme, basil,
   dill, or Italian parsley

PREPARATION
Preheat the oven to 450°F.

Place the bread slices on a baking sheet. Sprinkle with half of the cheese. Place the tomato slices on top of the cheese. Sprinkle lightly with salt, pepper, and the herbs. Top evenly with the remaining cheese. Bake until the edges appear toasted, and the cheese is melted, about 8 to 10 minutes.

Stuffed Portobello Mushrooms

This appetizer is the perfect balance of the meaty mushroom and rich, white cheddar.

Makes 4 servings

INGREDIENTS
4 medium Portobello mushrooms,
    about 4 to 5 inches in diameter
2/3 cup chopped red, yellow, and green
    bell peppers
1/2 cup thinly sliced green onions
1 1/2 teaspoons minced garlic
3 tablespoons finely chopped basil
2 tablespoons Tillamook butter
4 ounces Tillamook Vintage White Extra
    Sharp Cheddar cheese, crumbled
Salt
Freshly ground black pepper

PREPARATION
Preheat the oven to 425°F.

Remove the mushroom stems and chop. Sauté the stems, peppers, onions, garlic, and basil in butter in a medium skillet until tender. Cool. Add the cheese. Season to taste with salt and pepper.

Bake the mushrooms, cap-side-down, in a buttered baking pan for 15 minutes. Spoon the filling into the mushroom caps and bake for 10 minutes.

Sustainability

Our farmers live on or near the land they farm. They depend on it not only for their livelihood, but for their quality of life as well. Not surprisingly, it's important to them to protect and nurture these natural resources.
The limited pastureland in Tillamook County and our nearly 100 inches of rainfall a year often make meeting national, regional and local environmental rules and regulations more difficult than it is for other dairies. But that only makes us more committed to safeguarding area land and waterways.

Over the past twenty years, the cooperative responded to this challenge by starting innovative environmental projects such as the following:

Seven-Layer Dip

Everyone loves seven-layer dip! Watch this one disappear at your next party or get-together.

Serves 6 to 8

INGREDIENTS

1 large can (40.5-ounce) refried beans
3 avocados
3 tablespoons sour cream
2 tablespoons freshly squeezed lemon juice
1 cup shredded Tillamook Medium Cheddar cheese
1 cup shredded Tillamook Monterey Jack cheese
1 large container (24-ounce) Tillamook sour cream
1 package taco seasoning mix
1 1/2 tomatoes, diced
Sliced olives, for garnish
Freshly chopped green onions, for garnish

PREPARATION

Fry the refried beans in pan prior to adding to the recipe. Mash together the avocados, sour cream, and the lemon juice. Reserve.

Mix the cheeses together. Reserve.

Mix the sour cream together with the taco seasoning mix. Reserve.

Layer in a pan or glass dish in order listed, starting with the beans, then the avocado mixture, then the cheese, and finishing with the sour cream mixture.

Sprinkle the tomatoes, olives, and green onions over the top.

Serve with a large bag of tortilla chips.

- Fencing over 120 miles of streamside to keep dairy cows from damaging the banks.
- Installing over 200 alternate cattle-watering facilities.
- Planting native trees and shrubs to enhance existing streamsides and riverbanks and cool their waters.
- Working with scientists to implement environmental-enhancement projects.
- Participating in state and local environmental planning, including the Tillamook Estuaries Partnership.
- Working with local organizations to get coastal salmon back into their historical habitat by replacing problem culverts with bridges or fish-friendly culverts.

Risotto Fritters

A combination of traditional risotto and flavorful mozzarella.

Makes 12 fritters, serves 6 as an appetizer

INGREDIENTS

3 tablespoons minced shallots
2 teaspoons olive oil
1 cup Arborio rice
1 1/2 cups chicken broth
1 teaspoon salt
2 large eggs
6 tablespoons grated Parmesan cheese
Freshly ground black pepper
6 medium-sized fresh basil leaves, torn
 in half
3 ounces Tillamook Mozzarella cheese,
 cut into 12 (1/2-inch-thick) slices
2/3 cup dry, fine bread crumbs
6 tablespoons balsamic vinegar
Vegetable oil, for frying
Olive oil, for drizzling
Coarsely ground sea salt

PREPARATION

Sauté the shallots in olive oil in a medium saucepan until they are tender. Add the rice, and stir to coat. Pour in the hot broth, add the salt, and cover. Reduce the heat and simmer for about 20 minutes, or until the rice is cooked through. Allow the mixture to cool for 10 minutes. Mix in the eggs, Parmesan, and the pepper. Transfer the mixture to a pie plate and spread evenly over the bottom of the pan. Refrigerate until the rice has chilled slightly, about a half an hour.

To form the fritters, moisten your hands with water, and flatten one heaping tablespoon of rice in the palm of your hand. Place a piece of basil and a slice of cheese in the center. Fold the edges of the rice over the cheese, pressing firmly to form a 2-inch disk. Dredge in bread crumbs and chill for at least 30 minutes, or overnight.

Reduce the balsamic vinegar in a small saucepan over medium-high heat for about 4 minutes, or until reduced by half. Set aside to cool.

Heat 1/8 inch of oil over medium-high heat in a medium frying pan until hot, but not smoking. Sauté the fritters until they are golden-brown, about 3 minutes per side. Drain on paper towels.

Place the fritters on a serving plate and drizzle with the balsamic vinegar reduction and olive oil. Sprinkle with the sea salt to finish.

Portobello Mushroom Cheddar Melts

Serve these savory mushrooms atop thinly sliced, lightly toasted French bread, if desired. To serve as an appetizer, cut them into slices and arrange on a warm serving platter.

Serves 4 as a main dish

INGREDIENTS

2 tablespoons balsamic vinegar
1 tablespoon extra virgin olive oil
2 teaspoons soy sauce
1 teaspoon freshly chopped rosemary
1 small clove garlic, crushed
4 portobello mushroom, 5 to 6 inches in diameter (or 6 mushrooms, 4 inches in diameter)
4 slices Tillamook Sharp Cheddar cheese
Freshly chopped parsley, for garnish

PREPARATION

Preheat the oven to 375°F.

In a small bowl or a 1-cup measuring cup, whisk together the vinegar, olive oil, soy sauce, rosemary, and garlic.

Remove the stems and wipe the mushrooms with a damp cloth or paper towel. Place the mushrooms, gill-side-down, in a rimmed baking pan. Brush the caps lightly with the balsamic vinegar mixture. Turn the mushrooms over, and brush the gill-side generously. Allow to stand for 10 minutes. Bake for 4 to 5 minutes, depending on the thickness of the mushrooms. Top each mushroom with a slice of cheese. Bake for 1 minute more, or until the cheese is melted. Sprinkle with parsley and serve.

PREPARATION NOTE

Portobellos may be cooked on the grill. Cook for 4 to 5 minutes over medium direct heat, covered. Top with the cheese slices. Cover, and cook for 1 minute or more, or until the cheese is melted. Sprinkle with the parsley.

Cheddar Bread Sticks

"While this recipe may require more time than the Puff Pastry Straws, the results are worth it. The complex flavors of the Tillamook Cheddar, fennel seeds, and beer add new dimensions to the familiar bread-stick theme."

—Chef Ron Paul, Portland, Oregon

Makes 5 1/2 dozen crisps

INGREDIENTS

2 (1/4-ounce) package quick-rise, dry yeast
2 teaspoons sugar
3/4 cup warm water (110°F to 115°F)
3/4 cup vegetable oil
3/4 cup beer, at room temperature
1 teaspoon salt
2 cups grated Tillamook Sharp Cheddar cheese
1 tablespoon fennel seeds
4 1/2 to 5 cups all-purpose bread flour
1 egg, slightly beaten
1 tablespoon water
Coarsely-ground salt, or sesame seeds

PREPARATION

Sprinkle the yeast and sugar over the warm water in a large bowl and let stand until bubbly, about 10 minutes. Stir in the oil, beer, salt, Cheddar, and fennel seeds. Beat in 2 1/2 cups of the flour. Stir in enough of the remaining flour to form a soft dough.

Turn the dough out onto a lightly floured surface and knead until smooth and elastic, about 5 to 6 minutes. Place in a greased bowl and turn the dough greased-side-up. Cover and allow to rise in a warm place until it has doubled in size, about 30 minutes.

Grease 2 baking sheets. Punch the dough down. Divide into 2 parts and cut each part into 24 equal pieces. Roll each piece into a 6-inch rope. Place, 1-inch apart, on the baking sheets. Combine the egg and water. Brush the egg-water mixture gently over the bread sticks. Sprinkle the tops with the coarsely ground salt or sesame seeds.

Preheat the oven to 350°F.

Allow to rise in a warm place until slightly puffed, about 10 minutes. Bake until golden brown, about 30 to 35 minutes. Place on wire racks to cool.

Crispy Wonton
with Crab Salad, Melted Cheddar & Avocado Crème

Elegant, creamy, and crispy.

Makes 10 appetizers (30 wontons)

INGREDIENTS
30 (3-inch) round wonton wrappers
Oil, for frying

CRAB MIXTURE
20 ounces crab meat, well-drained
3/4 cup minced celery
3 tablespoons minced chives
4 teaspoons lemon zest
3/4 cup mayonnaise
2 tablespoons freshly squeezed lemon
 juice
1/4 teaspoon freshly ground black
 pepper

2 cups shredded Tillamook Medium
 Cheddar cheese

AVOCADO CRÈME
1/2 cup avocado pulp
1/4 teaspoon salt
1 tablespoon freshly squeezed lemon
 juice
1/4 cup cream

Freshly chopped chives, for garnish

PREPARATION

Fry the wonton wrappers in 350°F oil until they are light golden-brown. Drain on paper towels, and reserve. Combine the crab, celery, chives and lemon zest in a medium bowl. Stir in the mayonnaise, lemon juice, and pepper. Purée the avocado pulp, salt, lemon juice, and cream in a small bowl. Refrigerate until ready to use. Preheat the oven to 400°F.

Top each wonton with an equal amount of crab mixture. Sprinkle each with 1 tablespoon of shredded cheese. Place on a baking sheet in the oven and heat just until the cheese is melted. Remove the wontons from the oven and arrange them on a plate. Top with a spoonful of the avocado crème, and garnish with the chives before serving.

Beer & Cheese Spread

Three cheeses, beer, and pepper in a rich and creamy spread.

Serves 6 to 8

INGREDIENTS

4 cups shredded Tillamook Special Reserve Extra Sharp
  Cheddar cheese
1/2 cup crumbled Gorgonzola or blue cheese
12 ounces cream cheese, softened
2 tablespoons prepared horseradish
1/2 cup finely chopped white onion
1 tablespoon English dry mustard
1 bunch fresh chives, finely chopped
1 teaspoon red chili flakes
3 dashes hot pepper sauce (your favorite)
1 teaspoon salt
Several turns of freshly cracked black pepper
1/2 cup blonde ale
Crusty bread (such as sourdough), cut into bite-sized pieces, or
  assorted crackers

PREPARATION

Place all of the cheeses, the horseradish, onion, mustard, chives, chili flakes, hot sauce, salt, and pepper into a food processor. Pulse until the mixture becomes fairly smooth. Slowly pour in the beer until incorporated.

Pour the mixture into a suitable serving dish. Cover, and refrigerate until needed. Serve with the crusty bread and assorted crackers.

The first power curd mill for the Beaver Creamery, and possibly in the county. John Wyss, Mr. Perrin and Adam Schmelzer operate the mill. Addie Bunn stands in the background. 1910.

Glamorgan Cheese Rolls

A classy, cheesy little appetizer.

Makes 12

INGREDIENTS

1 cup shredded Tillamook Sharp Cheddar cheese
1/4 cup fresh white bread crumbs
2 tablespoons finely chopped leek
3 egg yolks
1 teaspoon freshly chopped parsley
1/2 teaspoon dried thyme
1 teaspoon English mustard powder
Salt
Freshly ground black pepper
1 egg white, slightly beaten
Dried bread crumbs, for coating
Oil, for frying

PREPARATION

Mix the cheese with the bread crumbs and the leek in a large bowl. Blend the egg yolks with the herbs, mustard, and the seasonings. Add this to the cheese/bread crumb mixture and mix well. Divide the mixture into 12 equal portions, and roll each piece into a 2-inch roll. Dip in the egg white, and roll in the dried bread crumbs.

Shallow fry until golden-brown on all sides. Drain on paper towels and serve immediately.

Confetti Cheddar Log

This is a great choice for make-ahead and take-along simplicity.

Makes one log

INGREDIENTS

1 (3-ounce) package cream cheese, softened
2 cups shredded Tillamook Medium or Sharp Cheddar cheese, at room temperature
1/4 cup chopped pimiento
2 tablespoons very finely chopped green bell pepper
Chopped pecans

PREPARATION

Beat the cream cheese until fluffy. Beat in the cheddar cheese. Stir in the pimiento and green pepper, blending well. Shape, to form a 7-inch log on waxed paper. Coat well with the pecans. Wrap and chill. Allow to stand at room temperature about 30 minutes before serving. Serve with assorted crackers.

Grilled Polenta Torta
with Tillamook Mozzarella Cheese

Start your evening off with a taste of Italy.

Makes 4 tortas to be served as an appetizer or first course

INGREDIENTS

1 small eggplant, cut into 8 (1/4-inch-thick) slices

2 tablespoons olive oil, plus extra for garnish

Salt

Freshly ground black pepper

1/4 cup purchased pesto

1/2 tube (about 9 ounces) pre-cooked polenta, cut into 12 (1/4-inch-thick) slices

2 medium tomatoes, cut into 8 (1/4-inch-thick) slices

4 ounces Tillamook Mozzarella Cheese, cut into 8 thin slices

Arugula lettuce, for garnish

SPECIAL EQUIPMENT

4 small wooden skewers and a small-holed grill rack

PREPARATION

Preheat the grill to medium heat.

Lightly brush both sides of the eggplant with olive oil. Season with salt and pepper. Grill the eggplant for approximately 3 minutes per side, or until soft. Remove the grilled slices from the heat. Place a small-holed rack on the grill to preheat.

ASSEMBLY

Spread 1 1/2 teaspoons of pesto on a slice of polenta, top with one slice of eggplant, one slice of tomato, and one slice of cheese. Repeat to make a second layer, and finish with a third slice of polenta on top. Secure with a small skewer through the center of each torta. Repeat with the remaining ingredients to make 4 tortas.

TO GRILL

Lightly brush a preheated grill rack with oil. Place the tortas upright on the rack. Cover, and cook for about 4 to 5 minutes, or until the cheese is melted.

Remove the skewers and serve with a salad of arugula dressed with extra virgin olive oil, sea salt, and black pepper.

Albacore Tuna & Smoked Cheddar
Cheese Stuffed Cherry Tomatoes

A complex mix of salty, savory, smoky—all packed into a juicy, sweet cherry tomato.

Serves 6 to 8

INGREDIENTS
1 pound fresh Oregon Albacore tuna
   fillets
1 lemon, thinly sliced
Olive oil, for poaching
1/4 pound diced smoked Tillamook
   Medium Cheddar cheese
2 tablespoons diced red onions
2 tablespoons minced capers
2 tablespoons chopped niçoise olives
2 tablespoons chopped cornichons
1 tablespoon chopped chives
1 1/2 cups lemon aïoli (recipe follows)
2 pints large cherry tomatoes, well
   washed
Salt
Freshly ground black pepper

LEMON AÏOLI
1 clove garlic
3 egg yolks
1 teaspoon Dijon mustard
1 1/2 cups canola oil
1/2 lemon, juiced
1 teaspoon salt

PREPARATION
Line a heavy-bottomed medium-sized skillet with the lemon slices. Sprinkle the tuna with salt and pepper and place on top of the lemon. Add enough olive oil to cover the tuna. Poach the tuna over medium-low heat until it is almost cooked through, about 3 minutes. Using a slotted spoon, transfer the tuna to a plate. Discard the lemon slices, and chill completely.

Flake the tuna into small pieces. Combine all of the remaining ingredients, and fold in the lemon aïoli. Season to taste with salt and pepper.

Cut the tops off of the cherry tomatoes and a small amount of bottom so they will stand upright without tipping. Remove the seeds and allow them to drain by turning the tomatoes upside-down. Fill with tuna salad.

PREPARING THE AÏOLI
Using a mortar and pestle, crush the garlic into a pulp. Add the egg yolks and mustard and mash into a paste. Once homogenous, begin to slowly drizzle in the oil. Use a plastic squeeze bottle with a tip to control the stream of oil. If the aïoli begins to thicken, add 1 teaspoon of lukewarm water. When all of the oil is incorporated, add the lemon juice and salt. Store, well-covered, in the refrigerator and use within 2 to 3 days.

CHEF'S NOTE
Since the eggs are raw, they must be certifiably fresh. If you are concerned about the threat of salmonella, use pasteurized eggs.

Created by Phillipe Boulot, Executive Chef
Heathman Restaurant
Portland, Oregon

Baked White Cheddar & Artichoke Squares

These little squares are a great snack or starter.

Makes approximately 3 to 4 dozen snack-size servings

INGREDIENTS

2 small jars marinated artichoke hearts
1 small onion, finely chopped
4 cloves garlic, minced or mashed
4 eggs
1/4 cup bread crumbs
1/4 teaspoon salt
1/8 teaspoon each: black pepper,
  oregano, and hot pepper sauce
2 cups shredded Tillamook Vintage
  White Extra Sharp Cheddar cheese
2 tablespoons freshly minced parsley

PREPARATION

Preheat the oven to 325°F.

Drain the marinade from one of the jars of artichokes into a frying pan. Drain the other jar of artichokes and discard the marinade or save it for another use. Chop all of the artichokes and reserve.

Sauté the onion and garlic in the marinade until the onions are transparent, about 5 minutes.

Beat the eggs in a medium bowl with a fork. Add the bread crumbs and all of the seasonings. Stir in the cheese, parsley, artichokes, and the onion-garlic mixture.

Turn into a greased, 7 by 11-inch or 9 by 9-inch baking pan. Bake for 30 minutes, or until set. Allow to cool in the pan.

Cut into 1-inch squares. These appetizers may be served hot, warm, or cold or even frozen for later use. (Thaw and reheat as instructed below.)

To reheat, place in a 325°F oven for 10 to 12 minutes, or reheat in the microwave.

Cold-Water Pink Shrimp Cocktail Au Gratin

Shrimp cocktail with an attitude!

Serves 6

INGREDIENTS

4 cups cold-water pink shrimp (approximately 1 1/4 pounds)

1 lime, zest and juice

1 mango, firm, but ripe, peeled, seeded, cut into thin strips about 1-inch long

1/2 cup jicama, cut into thin strips about 1-inch long

1/2 cup finely minced red onion

1/2 cup finely chopped cilantro or parsley

3/4 to 1 cup chili sauce

Red pepper flakes

Salt

Freshly ground black pepper

1 1/2 cups Tillamook Pepper Jack cheese

PREPARATION

Preheat the broiler.

Gently combine all of the above ingredients, except for the cheese.

Divide among 6 individual au gratin dishes, and top with the cheese. Place the dishes close under a broiler until the cheese melts, and serve immediately.

Chef Profile : Gary Puetz

"I grew up hearing my dad, an Old-World German, telling anyone who would listen that Tillamook Cheese was the best cheese in the world." says Chef Gary Puetz, also known as the Seafood Steward™. "And it really is—especially the Sharp and Extra Sharp Cheddars; they are an inspired gift from God! And Cheddar marries so well with my passion—seafood."

"But every Tillamook product is great, from the sour cream, butter, and ice cream to every kind of cheese. At any given time, I always have Tillamook products in my refrigerator. You really can't go wrong using high-quality, local products like Tillamook. Every person who makes the cheese has a personal investment in the product and it shows. Tillamook is simply the best!"

Chef Gary Rainer Puetz, seafood expert, has spent over fifty years in the food service and television shows, and serving on multiple boards. His love of seafood was developed during years of living in Newport, Oregon, where his hands-on experience working with fishermen soon made him a sought-after seafood specialist. Most recently, Gary has been working as the Executive Chef for Pacific Seafood, and writing his first cookbook.

LEFT to RIGHT:
Leisha, Kurt, Rudy Fenk,
Ryan (in Rudy's lap), Ruth
Fenk, Wendy, Terri (behind
tractor), Bart (behind tractor),
Josi (next to Wendy, black
shirt), Shelby (white shirt)

1940
9N Ford
owned by
Fenk Family
since new

Soups, Salads & Sides

Rudy Fenk, Bart and Kurt Mizee
Tilla-Bay Farms

"The Tillamook brand is synonymous with quality and consistency, and our performance as a business for a cooperative of our size is unmatched."

In 1918, Fred Josi emigrated from Switzerland and established a thirty-two-acre farm just west of Tillamook. Until the early 40's, the cows were milked by hand, and the milk shipped to the Tillamook Creamery. By 1951, the main plant in Tillamook had opened, and mechanical milking was being utilized at the dairy.

The farm is now managed by Rudy and Ruth Fenk, son-in-law Bart Mizee and grandson Kurt. Bart says that he likes the range of activities and skills involved in the job of a dairy farmer—from business management to animal husbandry and land management.

The family appreciates that the fruit of their labor has life-sustaining value to our customers. They say that "our hope is that future generations of our family can enjoy the dairy farm lifestyle."

Savory Southwest Bread Pudding

Usually bread pudding is for dessert. Mix it up with a veggie version, and take it to the dinner table.

Makes 10 servings

INGREDIENTS

2 cups corn kernels, fresh or frozen

2 teaspoons olive oil

1 1/4 teaspoons salt, divided

2 tablespoons Tillamook butter

1 1/4 cups chopped onion

2 teaspoons minced garlic

2 1/2 teaspoons ground cumin

1/2 teaspoon freshly ground black pepper

2 cups cream

5 large eggs

2 teaspoons Tabasco® pepper sauce

2 tablespoons freshly squeezed lime juice

1/2 cup diced green chiles

8 cups (3/4-inch cubes) day-old French bread (don't pack)

1 cup shredded Tillamook Pepper Jack cheese

1 cup shredded Tillamook Sharp Cheddar cheese

PREPARATION

Preheat the oven to 400°F. Butter 10 (6-ounce) ramekins.

Place the corn on a baking sheet, coat with olive oil, and sprinkle with 1/2 teaspoon of the salt. Roast in the oven for 15 minutes, or until the kernels begin to brown. Remove from the oven and allow to cool.

Melt the butter in a skillet over medium heat. Add the onion and sauté until soft. Stir in the garlic, and cook for an additional three minutes. Stir in the cumin, 1/2 teaspoon of the salt, and the pepper. Set aside to cool.

Reduce the oven temperature to 375°F. Whisk together the cream and eggs in a large bowl. Add the pepper sauce, lime juice, green chiles, and the remaining salt. Stir in the bread cubes, corn, and onion, mixing until all the ingredients are evenly distributed. Mix in the cheese.

Divide the mixture evenly among the prepared ramekins, and place them on a baking sheet. Bake for 25 to 30 minutes until golden-brown. Unmold and serve.

TO REHEAT

Preheat the oven to 400°F. Cover with foil, and reheat for 20 minutes.

Cheddar Scallion Biscuits

Serve these on the side of a hearty meal.

Makes 18 biscuits

INGREDIENTS

2 1/2 cups all-purpose flour

1 tablespoon sugar

1 1/2 teaspoons salt

2 teaspoons baking powder

1/2 teaspoon baking soda

1/4 teaspoon cayenne powder

1 stick Tillamook unsalted butter, chilled, cut into small pieces

1/3 cup thinly sliced scallions

1/2 cup shredded Tillamook Medium Cheddar cheese, plus 3 tablespoons, divided

1 cup buttermilk

2 tablespoons heavy cream

PREPARATION

Preheat the oven to 400°F.

Whisk together the first six ingredients in large bowl. Add the butter, and work the ingredients with your fingertips until the mixture resembles cornmeal. Mix in the scallions and the 1/2 cup of the cheddar. Stir in the buttermilk, and mix lightly, just until a loose dough forms.

Turn the dough onto a floured surface and knead lightly. Roll out the dough to 3/4-inch thickness and cut rounds with a 2-inch biscuit cutter. Re-roll the scraps, and cut the remaining dough. Place the biscuits on ungreased baking sheet, 2 inches apart. Brush the tops with cream, and top each biscuit with a pinch of cheddar. Bake for 15 minutes, or until the tops are golden-brown.

Storing Cheese

Cheese should be kept in its original package, covered tightly with plastic wrap after opening, and placed in the coldest section of the refrigerator (under 40°F). If surface mold develops, trim at least one centimeter off of the moldy section.

Shredded cheese loses moisture and develops mold more easily than chunks, because it has more surface area exposed to air. Store leftover shredded cheese in a resealable plastic bag and use within a few days. Use a utensil or pour directly from the bag to help prevent molding.

Tillamook Cheddar Cheese Soup
with Broccoli

Broccoli and cheddar—what better combination?

Serves 4 to 6

INGREDIENTS
1/3 cup Tillamook butter
1/4 cup all-purpose flour
4 cups chicken stock
1 cup finely diced yellow onions
1/2 cup finely diced celery
3/4 cup finely diced carrots
1 cup shredded Tillamook Cheddar
   cheese
1 cup cream or half-and-half
4 cups broccoli

PREPARATION
Heat the butter in a sauté pan. Slowly add the flour, stirring constantly, and cook on low heat. Continue stirring the roux until it starts to bubble, but do not allow it to brown. Mix the roux into the cold chicken stock and bring to a simmer, stirring constantly. Be careful not to burn the roux.

Sauté the onions, celery, and carrots, and add to soup. Purée the soup in a large blender until smooth.

While blending, add the cheese and cream, and continue blending until smooth.

Cut the broccoli into florets and blanch in hot water. Immediately shock them in ice water, and then drain. Chop coarsely. Add the broccoli to the soup as it is served.

SERVING SUGGESTION
Sprinkle with croutons and top with more shredded Tillamook Cheddar cheese.

Spicy Shrimp & Crouton Salad

Crunchy and spicy! Add some zip to your meal.

Serves 6 as a first course and 4 as an entrée

INGREDIENTS

3 tablespoons olive oil, divided
3 (1-inch-thick) slices French bread,
  crusts removed, cut into 1-inch cubes
Salt
Freshly ground black pepper
1/2 pound medium shrimp, peeled,
  deveined
1 jalapeño pepper, deseeded, minced
1 large avocado
2 medium tomatoes, diced to 1/2-inch
1/4 cup sliced green onion (bulb and 1
  inch of green tops)
1/3 cup freshly chopped cilantro leaves
1/2 cup shredded cabbage
1 cup Tillamook Garlic Chili Pepper
  Cheddar cheese, cut into matchsticks
1 medium lime, sliced
Lime-Cumin Dressing (recipe follows)

LIME-CUMIN DRESSING

2 tablespoons olive oil
2 tablespoons canola or vegetable oil
2 tablespoons freshly squeezed lime
  juice
1 tablespoon rice vinegar
1 teaspoon honey
1/4 teaspoon ground cumin

PREPARING THE LIME-CUMIN DRESSING

Combine the oils in a measuring cup. Whisk together the remaining ingredients in a small bowl. Continue to whisk while slowly adding the oil until well blended.

PREPARATION

Heat 2 tablespoons of the oil over medium-high heat in a large skillet. Add the bread cubes, and sprinkle with salt and pepper. Shake the pan occasionally until the bread cubes are toasted on all sides. Remove from the heat, and reserve.

Using the same pan, heat the remaining tablespoon of oil over medium-high heat. Add the shrimp. Season with salt and pepper, and sauté for 1 to 2 minutes. Stir in the jalapeño and cook for 2 minutes more, or until the shrimp are pink and cooked through. Transfer the shrimp to a large serving bowl.

Peel, pit, and dice the avocado to 1/4-inch. Add the avocado to the shrimp along with the croutons, tomatoes, green onions, cilantro, cabbage, and cheese. Drizzle with the dressing and toss to combine. Season to taste with salt and pepper. Garnish with extra slices of lime.

Giant Cheesy Double Corn Muffins

These versatile muffins are great for serving with chili. Just split the tops and spoon the chili in. You can also add 1/2 cup of minced green onion or crumbled bacon when adding the cheese to the batter.

Makes 6 large muffins

INGREDIENTS

1 (8-ounce) package (2 cups) shredded Tillamook Medium Cheddar cheese, divided
1 1/2 cups fresh, frozen (thawed) corn, or 1 (15-ounce) can whole kernel corn, drained
2 large eggs
2/3 cup whole milk
1 (8-ounce) box self-rising corn muffin mix (2 cups)
2 tablespoons sugar

PREPARATION

Preheat the oven to 400°F.

Grease a large (6-cup) muffin tin (1-cup capacity each). Measure out 1/2 cup of the cheese for topping. Reserve the remaining for the batter.

Pulse the corn in a food processor until it is coarsely chopped, about 10 pulses. Add the eggs and milk, and pulse to blend, about 3 pulses.

Place the corn-muffin mix in a large bowl. Add the sugar, the remaining cheese, and the corn mixture. Stir just until no lumps remaining. Spoon into the muffin cups, dividing evenly. (Batter will almost fill the cups.) Sprinkle with the reserved cheese.

Bake until a toothpick inserted in the centers comes out clean, about 18 to 20 minutes. Remove from the oven and cool on a wired rack for 5 minutes. Turn out and serve immediately.

Chicken & Cheese Chili

Serve this spicy chili with cornbread—or better yet, corn-on-the-cob!

Serves 6

INGREDIENTS

2 boneless, skinless chicken breasts,
  cut into 1-inch pieces
3 tablespoons canola oil
1 tablespoon Tillamook butter
2 large onions, diced
1/4 cup tomato paste
1 tablespoon chili powder
1 teaspoon cumin seeds
1 teaspoon marjoram
3 medium carrots, chopped
3 ribs celery, chopped
2 jalapeño peppers, deseeded, minced
1 (28-ounce) can chopped tomatoes
1 (8-ounce) can black beans, rinsed
1 (8-ounce) can red or pinto beans,
  rinsed
1 1/2 cups tomato juice
2 1/2 cups shredded Tillamook Medium
  Cheddar cheese
1/2 cup freshly chopped cilantro

PREPARATION

Sauté the chicken in a large pot with 2 tablespoons of the oil until the chicken is opaque. Remove from pot. Add the butter and remaining oil to the pot and sauté the onions over medium-high heat until translucent. Stir in the tomato paste, chili powder, cumin and marjoram. Cook the mixture about 10 minutes until it has become medium brown in color.

Add the cooked chicken, carrots, celery and jalapeños, and stir just to coat. Add the chopped tomatoes, beans, and tomato juice. Cook on low for 1 hour. Add more tomato juice if needed.

To finish, stir in 1 cup of the cheese until the cheese is melted. Spoon the chili into bowls and sprinkle each with the remaining cheese and cilantro.

Farmers deliver their milk to the Tillamook Creamery, circa 1916.

Cheddar, Pear & Walnut Salad
with Pear Vinaigrette

A sweet and simple salad.

Serves 6

INGREDIENTS
3/4 cup coarsely chopped toasted
  walnuts
2 firm, but ripe Bartlett pears, peeled,
  cored, sliced
6 handfuls Boston or Bibb lettuce, well
  washed, torn into large pieces
Pear vinaigrette (recipe follows)
1 1/2 cups crumbled Tillamook Vintage
  White Extra Sharp Cheddar cheese

PEAR VINAIGRETTE
1 firm, but ripe Bartlett pear, peeled,
  cored, quartered
1 tablespoon walnut oil
3 tablespoons olive oil
4 teaspoons sherry vinegar
1/2 teaspoon balsamic vinegar
1/8 teaspoon salt

TOASTING THE WALNUTS
Preheat the oven to 325°F. Spread the walnuts on a baking sheet and bake for 10 to 12 minutes. Allow to cool before chopping.

PREPARING THE PEAR VINAIGRETTE
Purée all of the ingredients in a blender or food processor.

PREPARATION
Toss the walnuts, pears, and lettuce with the dressing in a large bowl. Divide the salad among 6 plates and garnish with the crumbled cheese.

Cream of Potato & Cheddar Cheese Soup

This soup uses a fall harvest collection of vegetables.

Serves 4 to 5

INGREDIENTS

1 slice bacon, diced
1 tablespoon finely chopped parsnip
1 tablespoon finely chopped celery
1/2 tablespoon finely chopped rutabaga
1 mushroom, finely chopped
1 shallot, roughly chopped
2 cloves garlic, minced
2 cups chicken or vegetable broth
1/2 tablespoon finely chopped fresh
  basil
1 teaspoon finely chopped fresh
  oregano
1 teaspoon finely chopped fresh thyme
1/2 teaspoon finely chopped fresh
  parsley
1/2 teaspoon freshly ground black
  pepper
1 teaspoon salt
1 large russet potato, peeled, cut into
  1/4-inch pieces
1 small red potato, peeled, cut into
  1/2-inch pieces
3/4 cup heavy cream
3/4 cup finely grated Tillamook Medium
  or Sharp Cheddar cheese

PREPARATION

Sauté the bacon in a medium-sized soup pot over medium heat until well browned and nearly crisp. Remove the bacon pieces from the pot and drain them on a paper towel. Reserve.

Add the parsnip, celery, rutabaga, mushroom, and shallot and stir over medium heat for 2 to 3 minutes. Add the garlic, and stir for an additional minute.

Add the broth, basil, oregano, thyme, parsley, pepper, salt, and russet potato and bring the entire mixture to a slight simmer. Cover, and cook for 20 to 25 minutes over medium heat.

Mash the softened vegetables using a potato masher until there are no more large pieces and the soup is fairly smooth. Add the red potato and cream. Cover the pot, and simmer for another 15 minutes over medium heat. If the soup is too thin for your liking, continue to cook the soup to desired thickness before you add the bacon and cheese. If the soup is too thick, add milk after adding the cheese and bacon.

Remove the pot from the heat, add the reserved bacon pieces, and whisk in the cheese. Serve immediately in hot bowls.

White Cheddar Gourmet Crackers

The perfect snack! Eat by themselves or topped with more Tillamook Cheese. Great with any meal!

Makes 2 dozen crackers

INGREDIENTS
2 cups shredded Tillamook Vintage
  White Extra Sharp Cheddar cheese
1/2 cup Tillamook butter, softened
3 tablespoons Dijon mustard
1 tablespoon dry mustard
2 tablespoons brown mustard seeds
1 teaspoon salt
1 cup all-purpose flour

PREPARATION
Blend the butter and cheese in a food processor until smooth. Add the remaining ingredients, pulsing until just combined. Chill the dough, covered, for 15 minutes.

Preheat the oven to 350°F.

Roll the dough out onto a well-floured surface, 1/4-inch thick. Using a pastry cutter or a biscuit cutter, cut out various shapes…be creative!

Place the pastry shapes onto greased baking sheets. Bake until golden, about 12 to 15 minutes. Transfer the crackers to racks to cool.

Tillamook Aged Vintage Cheddar Cheese
Ice Box Crackers

You can use these as a substitute for tortilla chips with your favorite salsa.

Makes 2 dozen crackers

INGREDIENTS
1 cup all-purpose flour
2 tablespoons yellow cornmeal
1/4 teaspoon chipotle paste
1 teaspoon salt
Pinch of nutmeg
2 tablespoons Tillamook unsalted
  butter
1 cup grated Tillamook Vintage White
  Extra Sharp Cheddar cheese
1/4 cup milk

PREPARATION
Combine the flour, cornmeal, chipotle paste, salt, and nutmeg in a food processor. Add the chilled butter, and pulse until well mixed. Add the cheese and milk and mix until a dough is formed. Shape the dough into logs, wrap in plastic wrap, and chill overnight.

Preheat the oven to 325°F.

Cut off 1/8-inch thick slices of dough, and place them on a baking sheet. Bake for 20 minutes. Do not brown. Cool and serve.

Created by Leif Benson, Executive Chef
Timberline Lodge, Oregon

Smoked Salmon Salad
with Tillamook Garlic White Cheddar

A hearty salad with a blend of fresh vegetables and smoked salmon.

Serves 2 as an entrée or 4 as an appetizer

INGREDIENTS
16 spears asparagus, washed and
   trimmed
1/2 teaspoon olive oil
Salt
Freshly ground black pepper
1/2 pound new, red or white potatoes
4 ounces Tillamook Garlic White
   Cheddar cheese
2 teaspoons whole-grain mustard
2 teaspoons sherry vinegar
1/4 cup olive oil
1 heart of romaine lettuce
4 ounces (about 1 1/4 cups) smoked
   salmon, flaked
2 teaspoons capers

PREPARATION
Preheat the oven to 475°F.

Place the asparagus spears on a baking sheet and drizzle with the oil. Season to taste with salt and pepper. Bake for 5 to 8 minutes, or until the asparagus is tender. Remove the asparagus from the pan and reserve.

Place the potatoes in a 4-quart saucepan and cover with cold water by 2 inches. Bring to a boil, and add salt (1/2 teaspoon per quart of water). Reduce the heat to a simmer and cook, uncovered, for 10 to 20 minutes, or until the potatoes are fork-tender. Remove them from the water with a slotted spoon and drain. Allow to cool to room temperature. Cut into 1/2-inch thick slices. Using a cheese plane or vegetable peeler, shave the block of cheese lengthwise to make long, thin ribbons.

Whisk together the mustard and vinegar in a small bowl. Continue to whisk while adding the oil in a slow, steady stream. Season to taste with salt and pepper.

ASSEMBLY
Place several whole lettuce leaves on a plate.

Arrange 4 asparagus spears on each plate with equal portions of potatoes and salmon. Top with the cheese and sprinkle the tops with the capers. Drizzle the tops of each salad with dressing.

Dilled Cheddar Cheese Batter Bread

Great fresh out of the oven, or toasted the next day.

Makes one loaf

INGREDIENTS
3/4 cup milk
1 1/2 tablespoons dills seeds, coarsely chopped
1 tablespoon honey
1/4 cup canola oil
3 eggs, beaten at room temperature
2 1/2 cups whole-wheat flour
1 package dry yeast
1 1/2 teaspoons salt
3 1/2 cups packed grated Tillamook Sharp Cheddar cheese, divided
3 tablespoons chopped fresh dill

PREPARATION
Bring the milk, dill seeds, and honey to simmer in a small saucepan. Cool to 120°F. Whisk in the oil and eggs. Combine 1 1/4 cups of the flour, the yeast, salt, and 2 cups of the cheese in the large bowl of an electric mixer. Add the warm liquid mixture and the fresh dill. Beat for 3 minutes. Add the remaining flour and beat for 2 more minutes. Scrape down the sides of the bowl. Cover the bowl with plastic wrap. Let the dough rise in a warm, draft-free area until doubled in size, about 1 hour and 15 minutes.

Preheat the oven to 350°F.

Butter a 9 by 5 by 3-inch loaf pan. Do not stir the batter down. Spoon half of the batter into a pan. Sprinkle the remaining 1 1/2 cups of cheese over the top. Cover with the remaining batter and smooth the top with a spatula. Cover, and let rise in warm, draft-free area until the batter reaches the top of the pan, about 30 minutes. Bake until the bread is golden-brown and sounds hollow when tapped, about 45 minutes. Turn out onto a rack to cool.

Tillamook Cheese whole milk cheddar. In 1921, in an effort to brand Tillamook cheese to distinguish it from other cheeses, the word "Tillamook" was stenciled on the rind of each cheese. "Look for Tillamook on the rind," became the advertising slogan for Tillamook Cheese.

Buttermilk Cheese Bread

"These golden rolls will have difficulty surviving untouched before they cool so think ahead about doubling the recipe…or halving the number of guests! Don't be intimidated by working the cheese into the dough; the intensity of the Cheddar flavor will surprise you."
—Chef Ron Paul, Portland, Oregon

Makes approximately 2 dozen rolls, or 2 small loaves

INGREDIENTS
3/4 cup water
1 1/4 cups buttermilk
2 packages dry yeast
2 tablespoons sugar
2 teaspoons salt
4 1/2 to 5 cups all-purpose flour
1 1/2 cups shredded Tillamook Sharp
 Cheddar cheese
2 eggs, well beaten

PREPARATION
Warm the water and buttermilk together until the mixture reaches 100°F. Activate the yeast in the milk-water mixture, and add the sugar and salt, stirring until it becomes frothy. Add half of the flour, and the cheese, and beat until smooth. Add the remaining flour and knead to a soft, resilient dough mass.

Place the dough in a greased bowl, and turn upside-down. Cover with a towel and place in a warm area to rise. Allow to rise until doubled in size. Punch the dough down, and form into balls, or roll out and shape as desired. Place in a warm area to rise, again allowing the dough to double in size. Preheat the oven to 375°F.

Brush the rolls lightly with the egg wash just before baking. Bake until golden-brown. Serve warm.

Tortilla Chip Soup PICTURED

These two tortilla soup recipes are great because they're festive and easy to make.

Serves 4 to 6

INGREDIENTS
2 boneless chicken breasts, cubed
1 (28-ounce) can chicken stock
1 (32-ounce) can stewed tomatoes
1 (1.25-ounce) package taco seasoning mix
1 tablespoon cornstarch
1 bag of corn tortilla chips
1 cup Tillamook shredded Mexican Blend with
   Monterey Jack and Medium Cheddar cheese
1 bunch green onions, chopped
1 cup Tillamook sour cream

PREPARATION
Combine the chicken, stock, tomatoes, and seasoning mix and cook in a large pot until the chicken is done, about 30 minutes. Mix the cornstarch with a few drops of water to make a paste, and add to the soup to thicken. Continue to simmer for 15 more minutes.

Pour the soup into bowls and sprinkle liberally with tortilla chips, cheese, green onions, and top with a spoonful of sour cream.

Submitted by Tonya Jordan-Floyd
Tillamook Cheese Recipe Contest 2001
Berkeley, California

Sopa de Tortilla (Tortilla Soup)

Serves 2 to 4

INGREDIENTS
1 pound ground sausage
1 poblano chile
1 large piece of onion
2 pounds red tomatoes, chopped
Salt
Freshly ground black pepper
1 to 2 cups broth (chicken, beef, or vegetable)
2 cups heavy cream
4 cups shredded Tillamook Monterey Jack Cheese
24 corn tortillas

Submitted by Angeles Martinez
Tillamook Cheese Recipe Contest 2001
Los Angeles, CA

PREPARATION
Preheat the oven to 350°F. Have a large casserole dish or mold ready for baking and serving the soup.

Fry the sausage in a large pan with a teaspoon of cooking oil until browned. Add the chile and onion. Immediately add the tomatoes mixed with the salt, pepper, and broth. Leave on the burner to allow flavors to blend.

Take the sausage mixture off the heat and drain off the fat. Return the sausage mixture to the pan and add the heavy cream, then let it set. Heat a frying pan with oil until hot and quickly fry the tortillas, removing to paper towels to drain just when they soften.

Place a layer of 6 tortillas, two-by-two, in the casserole dish. Add the salsa mixture, then a layer of cheese, followed by another layer of tortillas, salsa, and cheese again, until all the ingredients have been used. Cover the dish with tin foil and bake for 15 to 20 minutes. Serve immediately.

Creamy Basil Gnocchi

Traditional Italian fare—simple and delicious.

Serves 6

INGREDIENTS
1 1/2 cups heavy cream or half-and-half
1 tablespoon freshly chopped basil
1/8 teaspoon freshly ground black
  pepper
1 teaspoon minced garlic
1/2 chicken bouillon cube
1 (1-pound) package gnocchi
1/2 cup Tillamook Finely Shredded
  Italian Blend with Mozzarella &
  Parmesan cheese

GARNISH
1 medium tomato, seeded and diced
3 basil leaves, cut into strips
1/2 cup Tillamook Finely Shredded
  Italian Blend with Mozzarella &
  Parmesan cheese

PREPARATION
Place the cream, basil, pepper, garlic, and bouillon in a 2-quart saucepan over medium- high heat. Bring to a low simmer, and cook for 10 minutes to thicken. Meanwhile, prepare the gnocchi according to the package directions.

Remove the cream mixture from the heat and slowly stir in the cheese. Add the drained gnocchi, and stir to coat. Garnish and serve in individual bowls.

Cooking with Cheese

When adding shredded cheese to hot sauces, use only moderate heat and a minimum of cooking time to ensure that the cheese blends and melts properly. A sharper cheese may have a smoother consistency than a younger cheese, which may become stringy.

Jalapeño Cheddar Muffins

Great with any meal!

Makes 6 large muffins

INGREDIENTS

2 cups all-purpose flour
1 tablespoon baking powder
1 teaspoon salt
1 1/2 tablespoons sugar
1 1/2 cups grated Tillamook Sharp
  Cheddar cheese
1/4 cup minced onion
2 small jalapeño peppers, deseeded,
  minced
4 strips bacon, diced, cooked
1/2 teaspoon crushed chiles
2 eggs
1 cup buttermilk
1/2 cup melted butter
1 teaspoon Dijon mustard

PREPARATION

Preheat the oven to 400°F.

Combine the flour, baking powder, salt, and sugar in a large bowl. Add the cheese. Sauté the onion, jalapeños, bacon, and chiles in bacon fat or oil. Whisk together the eggs, buttermilk, butter, and mustard.

Add the sautéed onions, and peppers to the wet ingredients. Add the wet mixture to the dry ingredients, being careful not to over-mix. Scoop into buttered or paper-lined muffin tins, filling them two-thirds full. Bake for 20 to 25 minutes.

Shrimp Cheddar Chowder

A different type of chowder—a perfect balance of sweet shrimp and sharp Cheddar.

Serves 6 to 8

INGREDIENTS

1 pound cooked shrimp
2 cups thinly sliced onions
2 tablespoons Tillamook butter
2 tablespoons all-purpose flour
1 1/2 cups water
2 cups diced potatoes
1 cup sliced celery
1 1/2 teaspoons salt
2 cups milk
2 1/2 cups grated Tillamook Sharp
Cheddar cheese

PREPARATION

Sauté the onions in butter until tender. Blend in the flour. Stir in the water, potatoes, celery, and seasonings. Cover and simmer for 20 minutes, or until the potatoes are tender. Add the remaining ingredients, and stir until the cheese is melted.

John Hoffman, cheesemaker at the Fairview creamery, stands at right. John Zumstein stands by the keg, and sitting, left to right, are Will Senn and Adrian Tinner. Circa 1910.

Butternut Squash & Cheddar Gratin

A savory dish that pairs nicely with pork or poultry.

Serves 6

INGREDIENTS

3/4 cup panko bread crumbs, or coarse, dry bread crumbs
1 3/4 cups shredded Tillamook Medium Cheddar cheese, divided
1 tablespoon Tillamook butter, melted
2 tablespoons olive oil
3 cups sliced onions
1 1/2 teaspoons salt, divided
1/2 teaspoon dried thyme
Freshly ground black pepper
2 teaspoons minced garlic
6 cups (about 2 1/2 pounds) butternut squash, peeled, seeded, cubed to 1/2-inch
3 tablespoons all-purpose flour
2 tablespoons freshly chopped parsley
1/2 cup chicken or vegetable stock

PREPARATION

Preheat the oven to 350°F.

Lightly butter a 2-quart (7 by 11-inch) glass baking dish.

Combine the bread crumbs, 3/4 cup of the cheese, and the melted butter in a small bowl. Reserve.

Heat 2 tablespoons of the oil in a medium frying pan over medium heat. Add the onions, 1/2 teaspoon of the salt, the thyme, and pepper. Sauté for about 15 minutes, or until the onions are lightly browned. Stir in the garlic and cook 1 more minute. Spread the mixture evenly in a prepared baking dish. Set the frying pan aside for later use.

Toss the squash with the flour in a medium bowl to coat evenly. Stir in the remaining salt, the parsley, and the remaining cup of cheese. Spread the squash mixture evenly over the onions. Place the frying pan over low heat, and add the chicken stock to deglaze the pan, scraping any browned bits from the bottom of the pan, about 2 minutes. Pour the stock over the squash mixture. Cover with lightly buttered foil, and bake for 30 minutes.

Remove the foil, top with the cheese mixture, and bake an additional 25 minutes, until the au gratin is bubbly and the top is lightly browned. Remove from the oven and allow to rest for 10 minutes before serving.

LEFT to RIGHT:
Pam, Steve, Meriah,
MacKenzie, Walt
Putt-Putt (the truck)

Sandwiches & Pizza

Steve and Pam Huber
Huber Dairy

*"We enjoy the challenges of a dairy farm. It was a good childhood.
It's a good life."*

In 1919, Casper Huber emigrated to Nehalem, Oregon from Switzerland, and purchased a dairy farm from the Lommen family. The farm was populated by Guernsey cows, and the milk shipped down the river to the creameries in Nehalem.

In those days, the river was the only option for transporting the milk because there weren't any developed roads. The farmers would load the heavy cans of milk onto flat-bottomed row boats and follow the tide the two miles down the river. For the return trip, they would have to wait until the tide was coming back in to safely return.

Steve and Pam were both raised on dairy farms, and they have raised all of their four children in the same manner. "It has established a great work ethic in all of us," they say. Steve and Pam Huber are the third generation of Hubers to farm their family's dairy.

Grilled Mexican Pizza
with Tillamook Pepper Jack Cheese

This is a fun appetizer for a small gathering. The pizzas are at their best when eaten directly off the grill. They are cooked one at a time but only take about 5 minutes. Once your guests have finished the first pizza the second will be coming off the fire!

Makes 4 pizzas

INGREDIENTS

1/4 pound chorizo sausage

12 ounces purchased pizza dough, divided into 4 equal pieces

Flour, for rolling dough

1 tablespoon olive oil

Salt

2 green onions, thinly sliced (bulb and 1 inch of the green tops)

1 medium Anaheim pepper, seeded, ribs removed, thinly sliced

1 medium tomato, diced

1 cup grated Tillamook Pepper Jack cheese

GARNISH

1/2 avocado, peeled, diced

2 tablespoons freshly chopped cilantro leaves

SPECIAL EQUIPMENT

Small-holed grill rack, wooden pizza peel or baking sheet

Tongs

PREPARATION

Remove the casing from the chorizo, crumble the meat and cook thoroughly on medium-high heat. Drain well, and reserve. Prepare the grill to cook the pizzas over indirect heat by placing the coals to one side or, if using a gas grill, turn one set of burners to low. Place a small-holed rack on the indirect side of the grill and preheat the grill to high.

On a lightly floured work surface, roll one dough piece into a thin round, about 6 inches in diameter. Repeat with the remaining dough pieces. Cover with a clean kitchen towel until ready to use.

Place one dough round on a lightly floured wooden pizza peel or the back of a baking sheet. Brush lightly with olive oil and season to taste with salt. Top with 1/4 of each: sausage, green onions pepper and tomato. Sprinkle 1/4 of the cheese evenly on top.

Slide the pizza off the peel or pan onto the preheated rack on the indirect side of the grill. Cover, and cook for 5 to 6 minutes. Remove the cover and, using tongs, slide the pizza to the direct side of the grill. Crisp the crust for about 30 seconds to 1 minute, taking care not to burn the pizza. Remove from the grill.

Assemble and cook the remaining pizzas, one at a time, flouring the peel or baking sheet for each pizza.

Garnish the hot pizza with diced avocado and chopped cilantro. Cut into 4 wedges and serve.

Cheddar Dijon Salad Pizzas

A tangy Dijon dressing makes an excellent flavor partner with sharp Cheddar cheese.

Serves 4

SALAD TOPPING
1/4 cup extra virgin olive oil
1 tablespoon Dijon mustard
1 tablespoon red wine vinegar
1 1/2 teaspoons brown sugar
1/4 teaspoon kosher salt
1 small clove garlic, crushed
8 to 10 cups (6 to 7 ounces) mixed leafy greens
1 cup shredded Tillamook Sharp Cheddar
   cheese

CHEDDAR PIZZAS
4 precooked pizza crusts, 8-inch diameter
1/2 cup chopped basil
3 green onions, sliced
1 teaspoon coarsely ground black pepper
3 cups shredded Tillamook Sharp Cheddar
   cheese

PREPARATION
Preheat the oven to 425°F.

Whisk together the olive oil, mustard, vinegar, brown sugar, salt, and garlic in a small bowl or 1 cup measuring cup. Toss greens with 1 cup shredded Cheddar cheese in a large bowl. Set the greens aside.

Arrange the pizza crusts on sheet trays. Sprinkle the basil, green onion, and pepper evenly among the pizzas. Top the pizzas with the 3 cups of Cheddar cheese. Bake for 8 to10 minutes, or until the cheese is melted.

Toss the greens with the dressing. Remove the pizzas from the oven and place on 4 serving plates. If desired, quarter the pizzas. Pile the leafy greens high on top of each pizza slice and serve.

Doing Things Differently

We're proud to be a farmer-owned cooperative because it means that the people who actually work the soil and milk the cows also own the business. That approach made sense to our founders nearly a century ago, and it still makes sense to us today.

We understand that ours is a unique approach in the industry. In fact, we have been defying trends since the beginning.

COW FEEDS: Our farmer-owners also rely on different feeds than many others in the dairy industry. Because virtually all of our farmland is permanent or semi-permanent grassland, any other kind of feed than grass would have to be imported into the county. So we've focused on supplying as much of our cows' forage needs as possible from our grass-based pastureland.

Tillamook Pizza Bianca

An elegant and flavorful choice, but still quick and easy.

Serves 4

INGREDIENTS
2 (8-inch) ready-to-serve pizza crusts
1 cup ricotta cheese
2 garlic cloves, pressed or minced
1/4 cup freshly grated Parmesan cheese
2 cups fresh spinach, washed, stemmed
1 cup red bell pepper, cut into 2-inch
  strips
2 cups shredded Tillamook Mozzarella
  cheese
1 teaspoon oregano
1 teaspoon basil
Dash of red pepper flakes

PREPARATION
Preheat the oven to 450°F.

Combine the ricotta, garlic, and Parmesan. Spread half of the mixture onto one pizza crust, leaving a 1-inch border. Place 6 to 8 spinach leaves over the white sauce. Scatter half of the red peppers over the spinach and sauce. Sprinkle with 1 cup of Mozzarella on top. Repeat the steps for the second pizza crust. Lightly dust each pizza with herbs and red chili flakes. Bake for 12 to 15 minutes, or until the cheese has melted and begins to brown.

NO ARTIFICIAL BOVINE GROWTH HORMONES: Our farmer-owners and contract milk suppliers for our cheese production are in compliance certifying that milk for cheese production delivered to our facilities in Boardman and Tillamook Oregon is from cows not supplemented with artificial bovine growth hormone (rBST). We adopted this policy in 2005, largely based on recommendations from our customers gathered during market and consumer research.

BREED MIX: The mix of cow breeds you will find on our farms is another way in which we've distinguished ourselves. Most are Holstein-Friesians, but you'll also find Jersey, Guernsey, and Brown Swiss. That's because our experience has taught us that these cows have higher protein and butter-fat levels in their milk, which produces more cheese.

Grilled Pizza
with Red Onion & Tillamook Smoked Cheddar Cheese

These pizzas can be served as the main dish, or use the slices as individual appetizers.
Either way, the smoky cheese and the flavor of the grill makes this recipe a great choice any time!

Makes 4 pizzas

INGREDIENTS

1 medium red onion, sliced to 1/2-inch rings
2 tablespoons olive oil, divided
Salt
Freshly ground black pepper
1 (12-ounce) purchased pizza dough, divided into 4 equal pieces
Flour, for rolling dough
4 teaspoons freshly chopped thyme leaves
1 cup grated Tillamook Smoked Medium Cheddar cheese

SPECIAL EQUIPMENT

Small-holed grill rack, wooden pizza peel or baking sheet
Tongs

PREPARATION

Prepare the grill to cook the pizza over indirect heat by placing the coals to one side. Or, if using a gas grill, turn one set of the burners to low. Preheat the grill to high.

Lightly brush both sides of the onion slices using 1 tablespoon of the olive oil and season with salt and pepper. Place the onion on a small-holed rack over direct heat and cook, turning as necessary until soft, about 6 to 7 minutes. Remove the onions from the rack and allow them to cool. Separate the onion rings. Move the grill rack to the indirect heat on the grill.

On a lightly floured work surface, roll the dough pieces into thin rounds, about 6 inches in diameter. Cover with a clean kitchen towel until ready to use.

Place one dough round on a lightly floured wooden pizza peel, or on the back of a baking sheet. Brush lightly with olive oil and season with salt. Top with 1/4 of the cooked onion rings, and 1 teaspoon of the thyme. Sprinkle 1/4 of the cheese evenly over the top.

Slide the pizza onto the preheated rack on the indirect heat side of the grill. Cover, and cook for 5 to 6 minutes. Remove the cover. Using tongs, slide the pizza to the direct heat side of the grill, and crisp the crust for 30 seconds to 1 minute, taking care not to burn the pizza. Remove from the grill.

Assemble, and cook the remaining pizzas, one at a time, making sure to flour the peel or cookie sheet for each pizza.

Cut the pizza into 4 wedges and serve.

Grilled Tuna Sandwich
with Cheddar & Tomato & Lemony Mayonnaise

Zesty mayonnaise adds some new flavor to the traditional tuna melt.

Makes 3 sandwiches

INGREDIENTS
1 (6-ounce) can tuna, drained
1/4 cup finely chopped celery
2 tablespoons mayonnaise
1 tablespoon freshly squeezed lemon juice
1/4 teaspoon lemon zest
6 slices French bread
1 cup Tillamook Finely Shredded Sharp
   Cheddar cheese
6 (1/4-inch-thick) slices tomato
Tillamook Butter, softened, for the bread

PREPARATION
Mix together the tuna, celery, mayonnaise, lemon juice, and zest in a medium bowl.

Lay 3 slices of bread on a work surface. Divide the cheese into 3 portions. Top each slice with 1/2 cheese portion, 2 tomato slices, 1/3 tuna mixture, and the remaining cheese portion. Top each with a bread slice, and press down gently. Spread each with butter. Place the sandwich, butter-side-down in the pan. Cook slowly until golden. Spread each top piece with the remaining butter, turn, and cook until the second side is golden.

Shrimp with Melted Cheese Sandwich

Really easy! That perfect throw-together appetizer or snack for an impromptu get-together.

Serves 4

INGREDIENTS
1 1/2 cups bay shrimp
4 teaspoons finely chopped celery
4 teaspoons finely chopped green onion
4 sourdough or French rolls
1/2 cup prepared tartar sauce
1 1/2 cups shredded Tillamook Medium
   Cheddar cheese

PREPARATION
Mix the bay shrimp, celery, and green onion together. Open the sourdough or French roll, face-up. Spread tartar sauce on each side. Top with the shrimp mixture and sprinkle the cheese on top. Broil until the cheese is bubbly

Smoked Salmon Panini

Tried and true flavors of the Northwest come together for a palate explosion.

Serves 4

INGREDIENTS
10 ounces smoked salmon
1 cup mayonnaise
1/2 tablespoon garlic-pepper seasoning
Zest of one lemon
8 ounces sliced Tillamook Vintage
   White Extra Sharp Cheddar
4 English muffins

AÏOLI
1 cup Tillamook sour cream
1 ounce freshly squeezed lemon juice
Zest of one lemon
2 teaspoons freshly chopped garlic
1/2 teaspoon salt
1 lemon, quartered, for garnish

SPECIAL EQUIPMENT
Panini grill

PREPARATION
Preheat the panini grill.

Break up salmon in a bowl with a fork. Add the mayonnaise, garlic pepper, and lemon zest, and mix thoroughly. Place one quarter of salmon mix on each of four English muffin halves. Top each with cheese. Top with the other half of the English muffin, and grill until the cheese is melted.

To make the aïoli, mix together the sour cream, lemon juice, lemon zest, garlic and salt in a bowl until well blended.

To serve, place the sandwich on a plate with a small ramekin of aïoli and garnish with lemon wedge.

Submitted by Zeb Johnson, Chef & Food Service Manager
Famhouse Café at the Tillamook Cheese Visitors Center
Tillamook, Oregon

Zeb says...

I wanted to create much more than a sandwich for our 100th Anniversary Cookbook. I wanted to bring together the flavors of Tillamook, so I went on a culinary vision quest around the Tillamook Cheese Visitors Center gourmet food department. There I found a Pacific Northwest favorite of mine, smoked salmon. Then I looked at the wide variety of Tillamook Cheese and I didn't have to stop and think for long which one would be the best complement to the salmon—of course, our Vintage White Extra Sharp Cheddar.

Combining these rich ingredients, I felt only one type of sandwich would do—a panini. Two hot grill plates pressing and toasting an English muffin, warming the salmon and melting the cheese to perfection, is the ideal cooking method for this recipe. I hope you enjoy it as much as we do at the Farmhouse Café.

Pork Burger on Focaccia
with Mozzarella & Arugula

A savory, Italian-influenced burger. Try something different with pork instead of beef.

Makes 4 burgers

INGREDIENTS
1 pound ground pork
4 teaspoons Tillamook butter, softened
4 (3-inch by 3-inch) squares focaccia bread, halved horizontally
Salt
Freshly ground black pepper
1 teaspoon olive oil
1 cup shredded Tillamook Mozzarella cheese
1/4 cup olive tapenade
1/2 cup roasted red peppers, sliced to 1/4-inch
1 cup baby arugula

PREPARATION
Preheat the broiler.

Butter the focaccia halves and toast under the broiler, butter-side-up, until golden. Reserve.

Gently form the meat into 4 (1/2-inch-thick) patties. Season with salt and pepper. Heat a skillet or grill pan over medium-high heat. Add the oil and swirl to coat the pan. Cook the patties for 4 minutes on each side, or until a thermometer inserted in the center reads 160°F. Top each patty with 1/4 cup of cheese. Turn off the heat, and cover until the cheese melts.

Spread 1 tablespoon of tapenade on each bottom half of focaccia. Place a patty on each and top with equal portions of red peppers and arugula. Top with the remaining focaccia halves and serve immediately.

Southwest Chili Burger

Delicious! From the zesty cilantro to the spicy pepper Jack, this burger has all the tastes of the Southwest in every bite.

Makes 8 servings

INGREDIENTS
2 pounds ground beef chuck
1/2 cup freshly minced cilantro
4 teaspoons ground chili powder
1 teaspoon ground cumin
1 1/2 teaspoons salt
1/2 teaspoon freshly ground black
    pepper
1 pound Tillamook Pepper Jack cheese,
    sliced thinly
8 hamburger buns

GARNISH
Guacamole Mayo (recipe follows)
Sliced avocado
Tomato
Onion
Lettuce
Pickled jalapeño slices

GUACAMOLE MAYO
2 avocados, peeled, pitted
4 teaspoons freshly squeezed lime juice
1 cup mayonnaise
1 teaspoon ground cumin
Salt
Freshly ground black pepper

PREPARATION
Preheat the grill.

Combine the meat, cilantro, chili powder, cumin, salt, and pepper in a large bowl, and mix well. Form 8 equal patties, about 3/4-inch thick.

Grill the burgers on an oiled grill rack over medium-hot coals until desired doneness is reached, about 4 minutes per side for medium. Arrange the cheese slices evenly over the burgers during the final minute of cooking time. Serve in buns with desired garnishes.

PREPARING THE GUACAMOLE MAYO
Place the avocados in a small bowl. Add the lime juice and mash until chunky. Stir in the mayonnaise and ground cumin. Season to taste with salt and pepper. Store in the refrigerator for up to 2 days. Makes 2 cups.

CHEF'S NOTE
For Southwest Chili Turkey Burgers, substitute ground turkey for ground beef, and add 2/3 cup very finely crushed tortilla chips to the burger mixture.

Crab Melts

It's quick, easy, and delicious and a family favorite. Tillamook Sharp Cheddar cheese gives a bite to the sandwich and highlights the silky luxuriance of the crab filling and the sweetness of the artichokes. Bits of red bell pepper add crunch and color.

Serves 4

INGREDIENTS
1 cup crab meat, picked clean
1/2 cup chopped cooked artichoke
   hearts
1/2 cup diced red bell pepper
2/3 cup sliced green onion, divided
1/4 cup mayonnaise
1/4 cup Tillamook sour cream
1 teaspoon grated lemon zest
4 large oval slices sourdough or French
   bread, toasted
6 ounces Tillamook Sharp Cheddar
   cheese, sliced

PREPARATION
Combine the crab, artichoke hearts, and bell pepper in a medium bowl. Add all but 2 tablespoons of the green onion, the mayonnaise, sour cream, and lemon zest. Mix well.

Spread the mixture evenly over the bread slices. Arrange the cheese slices over the crab mixture to cover. Place the sandwiches on a baking sheet. Place under the broiler until the cheese softens, about 2 minutes. Sprinkle with the remaining green onion.

Submitted by Priscilla Yee
Tillamook Cheese Recipe Contest 2001
Concord, CA

The R. Robinson Golden Cheddar display.
Left to right: Chas. Kunze, Mr. and Mrs. Zeimer, A.W. Bunn, R. Robinson and Gus Kunze. Circa 1905.

Classic Tillamook Cheeseburger

An all-American favorite! Even better with sharp Cheddar and all the right toppings.

Makes 4 cheeseburgers

INGREDIENTS

1 1/4 pounds ground beef
Salt
Freshly ground black pepper
4 slices Tillamook Sharp Cheddar cheese
4 Kaiser rolls, split and toasted
1 tomato, thinly sliced
Pickles, thinly sliced
Lettuce leaves, washed
1 medium onion, thinly sliced

PREPARATION

Form the beef into 4 (1/2-inch-thick) patties. Season with salt and pepper. Heat a large skillet or grilling pan on medium-high heat. Cook the burgers for 4 minutes on each side, or until a thermometer inserted in the center reads 155°F. Top each patty with a cheese slice, turn off the heat, and cover until the cheese melts.

Serve the burgers on the rolls with tomatoes, pickles, lettuce, onions, and your favorite condiments.

Gourmet Tillamook Grilled Cheese Sandwich

The "grown-up" version of a childhood favorite.

Serves 4

INGREDIENTS

8 (1/2-inch-thick) slices crusty country-style
  bread
3 tablespoons extra virgin olive oil
8 teaspoons tapenade (olive spread)
1 (8-ounce) bag (2 cups) shredded Tillamook
  Sharp Cheddar cheese
3 tablespoons freshly minced basil
2 roasted red bell peppers, julienne
8 slices bacon, cooked

PREPARATION

Brush one side of each bread slice lightly with olive oil. Turn over 4 of the slices of bread, oil-side-down. Spread 2 teaspoons of the tapenade on each slice.

Toss the cheese with the basil and divide this mixture in half. Reserve half of the cheese mixture. Evenly spread the cheese on top of the tapenade.

Top with the red peppers, bacon, and the remaining cheese mixture. Place the remaining bread slices, oil-sides-up, on top, making 4 sandwiches.

Grill the sandwiches over medium heat in large skillet until golden-brown, about 5 minutes per side.

Shrimp Ceviche Quesadillas

Ceviche is classic Latin fare. Here it is wrapped up in a tortilla and grilled to perfection!

Serves 6

INGREDIENTS
1 1/2 cups small cooked shrimp (about
  1/2 pound)
1/2 cup pico de gallo
3 tablespoons taco sauce
2 tablespoons freshly squeezed lime
  juice
2 cups shredded Tillamook Monterey
  Jack cheese
1 ripe avocado, peeled, pitted, cubed
6 (7-inch) flour tortillas
Tillamook sour cream

PREPARATION
Rinse and drain the shrimp. Press between paper towels to remove any excess moisture. Stir together the shrimp, pico de gallo, taco sauce, and lime juice in a small bowl. Cover and allow to marinate for 10 minutes.

Place equal amounts of cheese, avocado, and shrimp mixture on half of each tortilla. Fold over to enclose the filling. Place on a grill over low heat and cook for 3 to 5 minutes, or until lightly browned. Carefully turn and grill the other side. Serve with sour cream.

Did you know...?
Milk is very high in calcium and other good stuff, which is why it is so healthy for you. You would have to eat about two and one-half cups of broccoli, three and one-half pounds of cooked spinach, eleven and one-half carrots, sixteen pounds of peas, twenty-two oranges, fifty tomatoes, fifty slices of whole-wheat bread or one cup of turnip greens to equal the amount of calcium in two eight-ounce servings of milk.

Vegetarian Quesadillas

*Quesadillas are a quick and easy meal. They also are great appetizers—
make sure to have lots of salsa and sour cream on hand.*

Serves 4

INGREDIENTS
1 teaspoon vegetable oil
6 to 8 small flour tortillas
1/4 cup mashed ripe avocado
1 cup chopped artichoke hearts
4 tablespoons sliced green chilis
1 (8-ounce) bag (2 cups) shredded
  Tillamook Mexican Blend with Pepper
  Jack and Medium Cheddar cheese
1/2 cup Tillamook sour cream
1 cup salsa

PREPARATION
Heat the oil at low to medium heat in a pan large enough to fit a flat tortilla.

Spread the avocado, artichoke hearts, and chilis evenly on the tortilla. Sprinkle with the cheese.

Place another tortilla on top, and brown as the cheese melts. Flip the tortilla over using a large spatula and repeat the heating process.

Cut the finished tortilla into 4 to 6 pie-shaped pieces. Top each slice with a dab of sour cream and salsa.

Grilled Cheddar & BBQ Pork Sandwich

Making your own slow-roasted barbeque pork takes time, but the flavors will be worth it!

Makes 10 sandwiches

INGREDIENTS
2 pounds pulled pork
2 tablespoons olive oil
3 large onions, julienned
1/4 teaspoon salt
1/4 teaspoon freshly ground black
  pepper
1 1/2 cups chipotle barbecue sauce
20 (1-ounce) slices Tillamook Sharp
  Cheddar cheese
20 slices Texas toast-style bread
5 ounces Tillamook butter, softened

PULLED PORK
1 (4-pound) pork shoulder roast, at
  room temperature
2 teaspoons salt
1 teaspoon each: black pepper, brown
  sugar, garlic powder, paprika, thyme,
  oregano, chili powder
1/2 teaspoon cumin seeds

PREPARATION
Preheat the oven to 225°F.

PREPARING THE PULLED PORK
Combine the salt, seasonings, and cumin seeds in a small bowl. Rub the shoulder with the spice mixture. Place the roast on a rack in a large roasting pan and place it in the oven. Roast for about 9 hours, or until a meat thermometer reaches 175°F. Remove from the oven and cool slightly. Using two forks, shred the pork, removing any excess fat. Makes about 2 pounds of shredded pork.

SANDWICH ASSEMBLY
Heat the oil in a large skillet over medium heat. Stir in the onions, and season to taste with salt and pepper. Sauté until the onions begin to wilt. Reduce the heat, and continue to cook, stirring occasionally until the onions are soft and have caramelized to a rich golden-brown, about 20 to 30 minutes. Transfer to a bowl and reserve.

Combine the shredded pork with the barbecue sauce and reserve.

Preheat a heavy skillet over medium-low heat.

For each sandwich, use 2 slices Texas Toast, 4.5 ounces of shredded pork, 3 tablespoons of onion, and 2 slices of cheese.

Place one slice of cheese on a slice of bread. Top with the pork mixture, then the onion, then a second slice of cheese. Top with a second slice of bread. Spread butter evenly over the top slice of bread. Place the sandwich, butter-side-down, in the pan. Spread the butter evenly on the top slice. Grill until golden. Turn, and grill the other side until it is golden and the cheese has melted.

Tuscan Cheese Melts

These tasty, cheesy treats are filling enough to eat for a meal! You can also slice it smaller to serve as appetizers.

Makes 16 to 20 pieces

INGREDIENTS
2 whole loaves Italian bread, approximately 1 pound each
1/2 cup prepared balsamic vinaigrette dressing
1 (2-pound) package (8 cups) shredded Tillamook Medium Cheddar cheese
2/3 cup fresh basil, coarsely chopped
8 medium plum tomatoes, thinly sliced
Salt
Freshly ground black pepper
1/2 cup sliced, pitted kalamata olives

PREPARATION
Preheat the oven to 400°F.

Cut the bread in half lengthwise. Place the halves, cut-sides-up, on a baking sheet. Toast the bread for 10 minutes. Brush the cut sides of the bread with vinaigrette.

Toss the cheese with the basil. Divide the cheese into 4 portions, and spread evenly over each bread half. Arrange the tomatoes on the cheese and season to taste with salt and pepper. Scatter the olives on top.

Bake until the cheese melts, about 10 minutes. Cut each bread half into 4 or 5 pieces to serve.

SERVING SUGGESTION
Cut into slices and serve with mixed fresh salad greens tossed with vinaigrette.

Calzone
with Sausage, Mushrooms & Herbs

These little "pocket pizzas" are great for lunch!

Serves 4

INGREDIENTS
4 tablespoons olive oil, divided
1/2 cup chopped onion
2 cups sliced mushrooms
1 teaspoon minced garlic
1/2 pound Italian sausage
1/4 teaspoon freshly ground black
  pepper
1 (8-ounce) package (2 cups) Tillamook
  Finely Shredded Italian Blend with
  Mozzarella, Smoked Provolone, and
  Parmesan cheese
1 pound pizza dough
1 (16-ounce) jar prepared marinara
  sauce

PREPARATION
Preheat the oven to 400°F.

Heat 3 tablespoons of the olive oil in a large skillet over medium-high heat. Add the onions, and sauté until they are soft. Add the mushrooms, and cook until all the moisture has evaporated. Stir in the garlic, sausage, and pepper. Sauté until the sausage is cooked through. Drain the fat off, and place in a bowl to cool.

Once cooled, add the cheese and mix well.

Divide the dough into 4 equal pieces and roll into 8-inch circles. Divide the filling and place in the center of each circle. Fold in half and crimp the edges to seal. Brush with the remaining oil and cut a slit in the top of each calzone. Place on a baking sheet, and bake for 20 minutes, or until browned. Meanwhile, heat the marinara sauce to serve on the side.

The Tillamook Creamery, circa 1910. Jesse Earl, a farmer, sits in the wagon with the white horse, near the building. The dairy farmers would deliver their milk to the creamery closest to their farm in a horse and wagon. Creameries were the social center for each community. For many, it was the only opportunity to chat with people other than their family.

Roast Beef Sandwich

with Tillamook Smoked Black Pepper White Cheddar Cheese

These open-face sandwiches offer plenty of flavor, you can add more horseradish
if you really want some kick!

Serves 4

INGREDIENTS

1 medium red onion, sliced very thin,
   rings separated
1 teaspoon olive oil
1/4 cup rice vinegar
1 tablespoon freshly chopped parsley
Pinch of salt
Pinch of freshly ground black pepper
3 tablespoons mayonnaise
2 teaspoons prepared horseradish
4 (1/2-inch-thick) slices rustic style
   bread, lightly toasted
1 pound thinly sliced roast beef
20 thin slices Tillamook Smoked Black
   Pepper White Cheddar cheese

PREPARATION

Place the onions in a small bowl. Add the olive oil, and toss to coat. Stir in the vinegar, parsley, salt, and pepper. Cover, and marinate in the refrigerator for at least 2 hours. Combine the mayonnaise and horseradish in a small bowl.

Preheat the broiler.

Place the bread on a baking pan and spread with the mayonnaise mixture. Arrange equal portions of roast beef and cheese slices on each piece. Place under the broiler for about 1 minute, or until the cheese melts. Top with the marinated onions and serve.

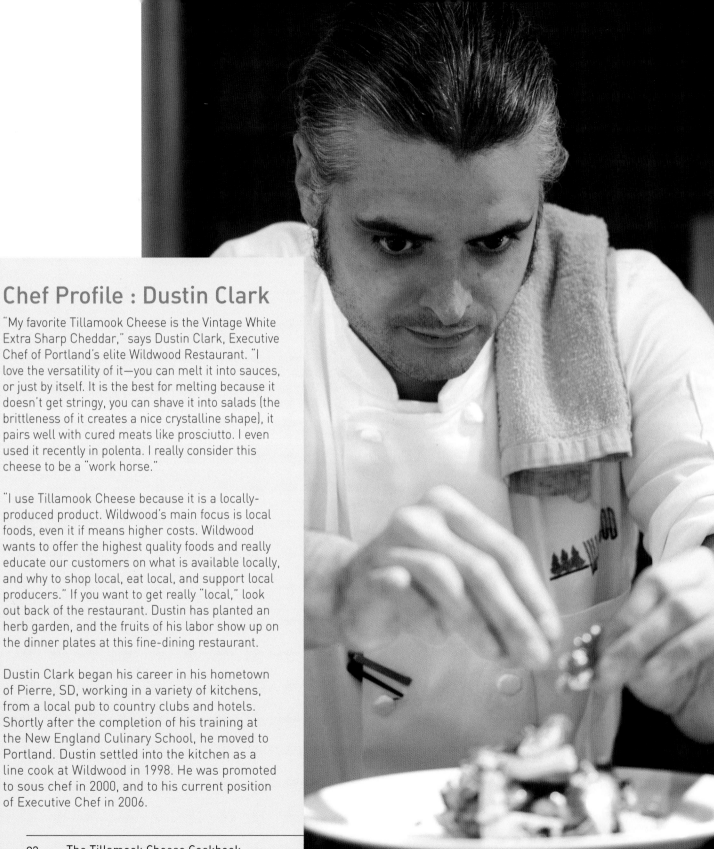

Chef Profile : Dustin Clark

"My favorite Tillamook Cheese is the Vintage White Extra Sharp Cheddar," says Dustin Clark, Executive Chef of Portland's elite Wildwood Restaurant. "I love the versatility of it—you can melt it into sauces, or just by itself. It is the best for melting because it doesn't get stringy, you can shave it into salads (the brittleness of it creates a nice crystalline shape), it pairs well with cured meats like prosciutto. I even used it recently in polenta. I really consider this cheese to be a "work horse."

"I use Tillamook Cheese because it is a locally-produced product. Wildwood's main focus is local foods, even it if means higher costs. Wildwood wants to offer the highest quality foods and really educate our customers on what is available locally, and why to shop local, eat local, and support local producers." If you want to get really "local," look out back of the restaurant. Dustin has planted an herb garden, and the fruits of his labor show up on the dinner plates at this fine-dining restaurant.

Dustin Clark began his career in his hometown of Pierre, SD, working in a variety of kitchens, from a local pub to country clubs and hotels. Shortly after the completion of his training at the New England Culinary School, he moved to Portland. Dustin settled into the kitchen as a line cook at Wildwood in 1998. He was promoted to sous chef in 2000, and to his current position of Executive Chef in 2006.

Grilled Cheddar Apple Sandwich

Sweet and savory elements bring out the richness of Tillamook Cheese in a most delightful way.

Serves 4

INGREDIENTS
3 apples, peeled, cored, sliced to 1/2-inch-thick
Olive oil as needed
8 slices of your favorite bread
Tillamook butter, for the bread
Caramelized onions (recipe follows)
4 (1-ounce) slices Tillamook Medium Cheddar
  cheese
8 strips thick-sliced bacon, fried crisp
Sage Pesto (recipe follows)

CARAMELIZED ONIONS
1 tablespoon Tillamook butter
2 yellow onions, finely sliced
1 clove garlic, minced
2 tablespoons balsamic vinegar
1 teaspoon Dijon mustard
Salt
Freshly ground black pepper

SAGE PESTO
1/4 cup coarsely chopped sage leaves
1/4 cup coarsely chopped parsley leaves
1/2 ounce toasted pine nuts
1 clove garlic, minced
Salt
1 ounce finely grated Parmesan cheese
1/4 cup extra virgin olive oil

PREPARING THE CARAMELIZED ONIONS
Heat a heavy-bottomed pan to medium high. Add the butter. Once the butter is sizzling, add the onions. Stir occasionally until the onions are nice and dark brown, about 30 minutes. Add the garlic and cook until tender, about 5 minutes. Add the balsamic vinegar and mustard. Season to taste with salt and pepper.

PREPARING THE SAGE PESTO
Place the sage, parsley, pine nuts and garlic in a food processor or mortar and pestle. Season with salt, and process until well-combined. Add the cheese. Slowly add the olive oil in a constant stream while the food processor is on.

ASSEMBLY
Brush the apple slices with olive oil and grill until they are just tender. Brush the bread with butter and layer with caramelized onions, cheddar slices, and bacon. Spread pesto on both sides of the bread. Toast on the grill as you would for a standard grilled cheese sandwich.

SERVING SUGGESTION
Serve with a simple tossed salad or crispy potato chips.

LEFT to RIGHT:
Kenny, Nicole (in front of Kenny), Carl, Nick, Linda, Kyla (in Linda's arms)

Macaroni & Cheese

Nick and Linda Hurliman
Lo-Land Dairy

"My dad and his dad cleared this entire land by hand…
it is amazing when you think about it."

The Lo-Land Dairy has been a Hurliman family operation since 1915, when Karl Hurliman moved from Switzerland and purchased 160 acres of bottomland in southern Tillamook County. He immediately set up the dairy, his sons working alongside him to help clear the land to take advantage of the fertile grazing land.

Today, the Hurlimans don't have to do much clearing of the land, instead focusing on the production of their milk and the care of the animals. Their hard work has paid off, with multiple quality awards from the Tillamook County Creamery Association.

Kicked-Up Monterey
Macaroni & Cheese

"Macaroni and Cheese is a favorite family meal, and for this version I added regional ingredients. I grew up in the San Jose area, so I included Monterey Jack cheese, shrimp, garlic, artichokes, and freshly picked lemons from my Dad's backyard tree in Cupertino."
　　　　　　　　　　　　　　　　　　　　　　　　　　　　　　　　—Priscilla Yee

Serves 4

INGREDIENTS

8 ounces uncooked radiatore or rotini pasta
5 tablespoons Tillamook butter, divided
1 clove garlic, minced
1/4 cup all-purpose flour
1/2 teaspoon salt
2 cups whole milk
1 1/4 cups shredded Tillamook Special Reserve Extra Sharp Cheddar cheese
1 1/4 cups shredded Tillamook Pepper Jack cheese
1 cup cooked small bay shrimp, peeled
1 cup quartered artichoke hearts, diced
1/3 cup chopped, oil-packed, sun-dried tomatoes, drained
1 teaspoon (or to taste) lemon zest
1/2 cup plain panko bread crumbs
1/3 cup coarsely chopped toasted hazelnuts

PREPARATION

Preheat the oven to 350°F. Cook the pasta in a large saucepan according to package directions to the al dente stage. Drain well.

Spray a 2-quart casserole with nonstick cooking spray. Melt 3 tablespoons of the butter over medium heat in a medium saucepan. Add the garlic, and cook for 30 seconds. Remove from the heat.

Stir in the flour and salt. Return the pan to the heat. Gradually stir in the milk and bring to a boil, stirring constantly, and cook for 1 minute more. Remove from the heat.

Stir in 1 cup of the Tillamook Extra Sharp Cheddar cheese, 1 cup of the Tillamook pepper Jack cheese, the shrimp, artichoke hearts, dried tomatoes, lemon zest, and the cooked pasta. Pour the mixture into a casserole dish.

Sprinkle the top with the remaining 1/4 cup of each cheese. Melt the remaining 2 tablespoons of butter in a microwave or saucepan. Add the bread crumbs, and toss to coat. Sprinkle the crumbs and hazelnuts over casserole.

Bake for 20 to 25 minutes, or until bubbly and crumbs are golden-brown.

CHEF'S NOTE

If you want a stronger lemon taste, just add more zest.

Finalist Name: Priscilla Yee
Macaroni and Cheese Recipe Contest, Regional Winner, 2005
Cook Off Location: San Jose, CA

The Everyday Macaroni & Cheese

What other dish is more loved by kids and adults alike than macaroni and cheese?
Try this quick-and-easy recipe that is sure to be a hit!

Makes 4 to 6 servings

INGREDIENTS
1 (8-ounce) package elbow macaroni
2 tablespoons Tillamook butter
2 tablespoons all-purpose flour
2 cups whole milk
1/2 teaspoon salt
1/8 teaspoon freshly ground black
   pepper
2 1/2 cups Tillamook shredded Medium
   cheddar, divided

PREPARATION
Preheat the oven to 375°F.

Cook the macaroni according to package directions to the al dente stage. Drain and reserve.

Meanwhile, melt the butter in a medium saucepan, and whisk in the flour. Cook, whisking constantly, for 3 minutes until smooth. Gradually stir in the milk, and bring just to a boil while stirring continuously. Reduce the heat, and simmer, whisking often, until the sauce thickens slightly, about 4 to 5 minutes. Add the salt, pepper, and 2 cups of the cheese, stirring constantly until the cheese melts. Remove the pan from the heat, and fold in the reserved pasta. Pour the mixture into a prepared baking dish, and top with the remaining cheese.

Bake for 15 to 20 minutes, or until the cheese is bubbly and the top is going to brown. Allow to stand for 5 minutes before serving.

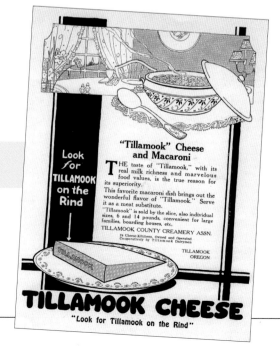

1923 ad for Tillamook Cheese featuring "Tillamook" cheese and macaroni.

Cajun Shrimp, Shells & Cheese

The cheeses in this dish make an amazing smooth, rich flavor. It's perfect for entertaining a crowd.

Serves 8 to 10

INGREDIENTS

1 pound small shrimp (41 to 50 per pound), shelled, deveined

1 1/2 cups coarse, fresh bread crumbs (from ciabatta or firm white bread)

6 tablespoons Tillamook unsalted butter, divided

1/2 cup shredded Parmesan cheese

2 tablespoons finely chopped parsley

1 tablespoon plus 1/2 teaspoon salt, divided

1 pound uncooked large-shell pasta

1/2 cup chopped onion

2 teaspoons minced garlic

1 to 2 jalapeño peppers, deseeded, finely chopped

1/4 cup all-purpose flour

2 cups whole milk

2 cups heavy cream or half-and-half

1 cup shredded Tillamook Vintage White Medium Cheddar cheese

1 cup shredded Tillamook Sharp Cheddar cheese

1 cup shredded Tillamook Colby Jack cheese

1 cup shredded Tillamook Swiss cheese

1/2 teaspoon freshly ground black pepper

1 teaspoon Tabasco® pepper sauce

1/2 cup chopped, cooked bacon (6 ounces uncooked bacon)

PREPARATION

Preheat the oven to 350°F. Lightly butter a 9 by 13-inch shallow baking dish.

To make the topping, combine the bread crumbs, 2 tablespoons of melted butter, the Parmesan, and parsley in a small bowl. Reserve.

Bring 5 quarts of water to a boil in a large pot. Add 1 tablespoon of the salt and the pasta. Cook according to package directions, stirring occasionally, to the al dente stage. Drain the pasta in a colander, and transfer to a large bowl. Reserve.

Prepare the sauce while the pasta is cooking. Melt 4 tablespoons of the butter in a large saucepan, over medium heat. Whisk in the onion, and cook until softened, about 3 to 5 minutes. Whisk in the garlic and the jalapeño, and cook for 1 minute. Add the flour, and cook for 3 minutes, whisking constantly. Gradually add the milk and cream, and whisk constantly until the mixture comes just to a boil. Reduce the heat and simmer, stirring often, until the sauce thickens slightly, about 4 to 5 minutes. Add the cheeses, stirring until the cheese is thoroughly melted.

Over low heat, stir in the salt, pepper, pepper sauce, bacon, and shrimp. Cook just until the shrimp is pink, about 2 minutes. Add the sauce to the pasta and fold to combine. Pour the hot mixture into a prepared baking dish. Immediately top with the crumb mixture and broil, about 4 to 5 inches from the heat, until golden-brown. Allow to stand 5 minutes before serving.

CHEF'S NOTE

To make fresh bread crumbs, tear rolls of bread slices into large pieces, and place in a food processor. Pulse until the crumbs have reached the desired texture. Two slices of sandwich bread or 1 medium-sized roll makes about 1 cup of coarse crumbs. When measuring soft bread crumbs, pile loosely in the measuring cup.

Cheesy Pasta & Lobster Bake
Macaroni & Cheese

Macaroni and Cheese is not just a weeknight classic. The rich and creamy cheese sauce and decadent lobster make this a fancy dinner party favorite!

Serves 6

INGREDIENTS

1 pound lobster meat, cleaned, chopped
7 1/2 tablespoons Tillamook butter, divided
4 tablespoons all-purpose flour
2 cups half-and-half
1 1/4 cups shredded Tillamook Sharp Cheddar cheese
1 1/4 cups shredded Tillamook Monterey Jack cheese
1 1/2 cups shredded Parmigiano-Reggiano cheese, divided
1/2 cup shredded Gruyère cheese
1 teaspoon minced garlic
1 3/4 teaspoons salt, divided
3/4 teaspoon freshly ground black pepper
1 pound packaged, dry gnocchi-shaped pasta
Nonstick cooking spray
1/3 cup seasoned bread crumbs
2 teaspoons chopped green onions, green tops only
1/2 teaspoon paprika
1/2 teaspoon dried basil
1/2 teaspoon dried thyme

PREPARATION

Preheat the oven to 350°F.

For the béchamel sauce, melt 4 tablespoons of the butter in a medium saucepan over low heat. Slowly add the flour, stirring to combine. Cook, stirring constantly, for 3 minutes. Increase the heat to medium and, with a wire whisk, gradually add the half-and-half. Cook for 3 to 5 minutes, or until the sauce has thickened, stirring often. Remove from the heat, and add 1/2 cup of the Parmigiano-Reggiano, 1/2 cup Gruyère cheese, the garlic, 3/4 teaspoon of the salt, and the pepper. Stir until the cheese is melted and well combined. Cover and reserve.

Fill a large pan with water and the remaining salt, and bring to a rolling boil over high heat. Add the pasta, return to a boil, and reduce the heat to a low boil. Cook for about 8 to 10 minutes, to the al dente stage. Drain the pasta and return to the pan. Add the béchamel sauce and 2 tablespoons of the butter. Stir until well combined. Reserve.

Combine the Tillamook Sharp Cheddar and Monterey Jack cheeses, and 1 cup of the Parmigiano-Reggiano cheese in a large bowl.

Spray a 3-quart baking dish with nonstick cooking spray. Place one half of the pasta in the baking dish. Top with half of the mixed cheeses. Top with the other half of the pasta, followed by the remaining mixed cheeses. Bake for 35 to 40 minutes, or until the macaroni and cheese is visibly bubbling and hot.

While the pasta is baking, combine the remaining butter and the lobster meat in a medium saucepan, over medium-low heat for 3 minutes, or until the lobster is heated through. Remove from the heat and add the bread crumbs, green onions, paprika, basil, and thyme, and the remaining Parmigiano-Reggiano cheese. Toss lightly to combine.

Remove the dish from the oven and evenly spoon the lobster mixture over the top of the pasta. Meanwhile, preheat the broiler.

Return the dish to the oven. Allow to broil for 10 to 12 minutes, or until the top is golden-brown. Allow to stand for 5 minutes before serving.

Submitted by Ann Jones
Macaroni and Cheese Recipe Contest, Regional Winner, 2005
Cook Off Location: Denver, CO

Simply Italian Macaroni & Cheese

The pancetta and Mozzarella give this a distinctly Italian taste.

Serves 8 to10

INGREDIENTS

7 tablespoons Tillamook unsalted butter, divided

1 1/2 cups panko or coarse dry bread crumbs.

1 1/2 cups shredded Parmesan cheese, divided

4 teaspoons salt

1 pound dry medium-shell pasta

1 tablespoon olive oil

6 ounces pancetta, cut into 1/4-inch cubes

1 tablespoon minced garlic

1/4 cup all-purpose flour

3 cups whole milk

1/2 teaspoon nutmeg

1/2 teaspoon freshly ground black pepper

2 cups shredded Tillamook Vintage White Medium Cheddar cheese

2 cups shredded Tillamook Mozzarella cheese

8 ounces Tillamook Mozzarella cheese, cut into 1/2-inch cubes

2 tablespoons freshly chopped basil

PREPARING THE CARAMELIZED ONIONS

Preheat the oven to 350°F. Lightly butter a 9 by 13-inch shallow baking dish.

Melt 3 tablespoons of the butter. Combine the bread crumbs, 1/2 cup of the Parmesan, and the melted butter in a small bowl. Reserve.

Bring 5 quarts of water to a boil in a large pot. Add the salt and the pasta. Cook according to package directions stirring occasionally, to the al dente stage. Drain the pasta in a colander and reserve.

Prepare the sauce while the pasta is cooking. Heat the oil over medium-low heat in a large saucepan. Add the pancetta and sauté until the pancetta begins to brown, about 8 minutes. Stir in the garlic and cook for 1 minute. Increase the heat to medium, and add the remaining butter. When the butter has melted, stir in the flour and cook, stirring constantly, for 3 minutes. Gradually add the milk and bring just to a boil, stirring constantly. Reduce the heat, add the nutmeg and pepper and simmer, stirring often, until the sauce thickens slightly, about 4 to 5 minutes.

Add the Cheddar, Mozzarella, and the remaining Parmesan. Stir until the cheese is melted. Remove the pan from the heat and gently fold in the pasta. Add the cubed Mozzarella and basil. Stir gently, until well combined.

Spread the mixture into a prepared baking dish. Top with the bread crumb mixture. Bake for 35 to 40 minutes, or until the cheese is bubbly, and the top begins to brown. Allow to stand for 5 minutes before serving.

Submitted by Debbie Reid
Macaroni and Cheese Recipe Contest, Regional Finalist, 2007
Cook Off Location: Chicago, IL

Truffle-Scented Mac & Cheese
with Crisped Pancetta

Tossing pasta with truffle oil and adding crisped pancetta jazzed up this recipe and gave it some style and sophistication.

Serves 8 or more

INGREDIENTS

8 ounces uncooked small elbow macaroni or mini penne
1 tablespoon white truffle oil
4 ounces pancetta or slab bacon, finely diced
3 ounces button mushrooms, sliced
2 3/4 cups whole milk
1/4 cup butter
1/4 cup all-purpose flour
1/2 teaspoon salt
1/4 teaspoon freshly ground white pepper
1/8 teaspoon each: ground nutmeg, ground red pepper
2 1/2 cups shredded Tillamook Special Reserve Extra Sharp Cheddar cheese
3/4 cup shredded Gruyére cheese
1 cup shredded Tillamook Vintage White Extra Sharp Smoked Cheddar cheese, divided
4 tablespoons snipped fresh chives, divided
6 tablespoons panko bread crumbs
Long chive strips for garnish (optional)

PREPARATION

Boil the macaroni in a large saucepan of salted water to the al dente stage. Drain well. Transfer to a large bowl and toss with the truffle oil.

In a medium nonstick skillet over medium heat add the pancetta and sauté until golden-brown, about 4 minutes. Add the mushrooms and sauté until tender, about 3 minutes. Drain on paper towels. Set aside and keep warm.

Bring the milk to a simmer in a medium saucepan over medium-high heat. Remove from the heat. Melt the butter in a large saucepan over medium heat. Add the flour and stir until the roux is a pale golden color, about 1 minute. Whisk in the hot milk. Cook over medium heat until thickened, stirring frequently, about 2 minutes. Remove from the heat and stir in the salt, white pepper, nutmeg, and red pepper. Add the Cheddar, Gruyére, and 1/2 cup of the Extra Sharp Smoked White Cheddar, and 3 tablespoons of chives. Stir until melted. Add the elbow macaroni and pancetta mixture to the cheese sauce and toss to coat.

Preheat the broiler.

Divide the cheese mixture among 6 (1 1/2-cup) soufflé baking cups measuring 3 3/4 by 2 1/2-inch or 4 1/2 by 2-inch. Sprinkle each with 1 heaping tablespoon Extra Sharp Smoked White Cheddar and 1 tablespoon of bread crumbs. Sprinkle with the remaining chives. Broil until the bread crumbs are golden-brown, about 1 minute. Garnish with chive strips, or as desired.

Submitted by Gloria Bradley
Macaroni and Cheese Recipe Contest, Regional Winner, 2006
Cook Off Location: Chicago, IL

Apple White Cheddar & Gruyère
Macaroni & Cheese

"When I heard about the Tillamook Macaroni and Cheese contest, I set out to create a recipe that would be unique. After some thought, I had a couple of ideas, and was off to the store for ingredients. I saw a display for apple cider, and it hit me that apples and Cheddar go really well together, so I abandoned my other ideas, and set out to make a recipe including apple cider. I finally found a balance of ingredients I was happy with." —Tim Hutchinson

Serves 8 or more

INGREDIENTS
6 slices French bread
6 tablespoons unsalted butter, divided
2 cups milk
1 1/4 cups heavy cream
3/4 cup apple cider
6 tablespoons flour
2 tablespoons, plus 1/2 teaspoon salt
1/4 teaspoon freshly ground black pepper
1/4 teaspoon nutmeg
1/4 teaspoon cayenne pepper
1 tablespoon Dijon mustard
3 1/2 cups shredded Tillamook Vintage White Extra Sharp Cheddar cheese
1 cup shredded Gruyère cheese
3 to 4 quarts water
4 cups medium shell pasta
Granny Smith apple wedges, for garnish
Sprig of mint, for garnish

PREPARATION

Preheat the oven to 375°F. Butter a 13 by 9-inch or 3-quart casserole dish. Remove the crust from the French bread, cut into 1/2-inch cubes, and place in a bowl. Melt 2 tablespoons of butter over medium heat. Pour the melted butter over the bread. Toss to coat. Put the bread cubes into a food processor and process until fine crumbs form. Reserve the bread crumbs.

In a medium saucepan over medium heat, heat the milk, cream, and apple cider until hot.

While the milk mixture is heating, melt the remaining 4 tablespoons of butter in a large, high-sided skillet, over medium heat. When the butter is melted and bubbling, add the flour. Cook, stirring constantly, for 1 minute.

Pour the hot-milk mixture slowly into a skillet with the flour-butter mixture, whisking constantly. Continue cooking and whisking over medium heat until the sauce bubbles and becomes thick.

Remove from the heat and stir in the salt, pepper, nutmeg, cayenne pepper, mustard, 2 1/2 cups of the Cheddar, and 1/2 cup of the Gruyère. Combine, and set aside.

Fill a large saucepan with 3 to 4 quarts of water, and add the remaining 2 tablespoons of salt and bring to a boil. Add the pasta and cook to the al dente stage. Pour the pasta into a colander, and rinse under cold water. Drain well.

Stir the pasta into the cheese sauce and transfer to a prepared casserole dish. Sprinkle the remaining 1 1/2 cups of cheese over the pasta, and top with the bread crumbs, covering the top. Bake for about 30 minutes, or until golden-brown on top.

Garnish with a sprig of mint and the apple wedges.

Submitted by Tim Hutchinson
Macaroni and Cheese Recipe Contest, Regional Winner, 2006
Cook Off Location: Seattle, WA

Irresistible Macaroni & Cheese

A twist on traditional Macaroni and Cheese, this uses a bit of mustard and horseradish for a kick.

Serves 8

INGREDIENTS

1 1/2 cups panko or coarse dry bread crumbs

7 tablespoons Tillamook unsalted butter, divided

1 tablespoon sesame seeds

1 tablespoon of salt

12 ounces uncooked medium elbow macaroni

1/2 cup finely chopped onion

3 tablespoons all-purpose flour

2 cups whole milk

1 cup half-and-half

2 teaspoons Dijon mustard

2 teaspoons creamy horseradish

1 teaspoon paprika

1 teaspoon salt

1/4 teaspoon freshly ground black pepper

1 (8-ounce) package shredded Tillamook Sharp Cheddar cheese

1 cup shredded Tillamook Colby Jack cheese

1 cup shredded Tillamook Swiss cheese

PREPARATION

Preheat the oven to 350°F. Lightly butter a 9 by 13-inch shallow baking dish.

Combine the bread crumbs, 3 tablespoons of melted butter and the sesame seeds in a small bowl. Reserve.

Bring 4 quarts of water to a boil in a large pot. Add 1 tablespoon of salt and the pasta. Cook, stirring occasionally, according to package directions, to the al dente stage. Drain the pasta in a colander and reserve.

Prepare the sauce while the pasta is cooking. Melt the remaining butter in a large saucepan over medium heat. Stir in the onions and sauté for 3 to 5 minutes, or until softened. Whisk in the flour and cook for 3 minutes, whisking constantly. Gradually add the milk and half-and-half, and bring just to a boil, whisking constantly. Reduce the heat and simmer, whisking often, until the sauce thickens slightly, about 4 to 5 minutes. Whisk in the mustard, horseradish, paprika, salt, and pepper. Add the cheeses, stirring until it has melted. Remove the pan from the heat and gently fold in the macaroni. Pour the mixture into a prepared baking dish, and top with the bread crumb mixture.

Bake for 25 to 30 minutes until the cheese is bubbly, and the top begins to brown.

Remove from the oven and allow to stand for 5 minutes before serving.

Jumbo Shell Pasta
Stuffed with White Cheddar & Chicken Macaroni

"The idea for my recipe hit me when I saw two boxes of jumbo shell pasta and baby-shell pasta next to each other on the grocery store shelf. I had a "lightbulb moment" and decided to stuff the small shells into the big shells. I bought some Tillamook White Cheddar cheese, ran home, and put the dish together. It turned out great the first time, so I submitted it, and promptly forgot all about it. No one was more surprised than me when they called my name as the grand-prize winner!"

—Lorie Roach

Serves 8 or more

INGREDIENTS

6 ounces uncooked small shell
  macaroni noodles
12 ounces uncooked jumbo shell
  macaroni noodles
1/4 cup Tillamook salted butter
1/4 cup all-purpose flour
2 cups whole milk
1 cup half-and-half
1 teaspoon salt
1 teaspoon cracked black pepper
4 cups shredded Tillamook Vintage
  White Extra Sharp Cheddar cheese,
  divided
3/4 cup oil-packed sun-dried tomatoes,
  drained, chopped
2 cups shredded, cooked chicken
Nonstick cooking spray
2 tablespoons Tillamook butter, melted
1 cup finely crushed cornflakes

PREPARATION

Preheat the oven to 400°F.

Cook both types of macaroni noodles in large saucepans, separately, according to package directions to the al dente stage. Immediately rinse with cold water to stop the cooking process. Drain and reserve.

Melt the butter in a large heavy saucepan over medium to high heat. Add the flour and whisk for 1 minute. Gradually whisk in the milk and half-and-half, and continue to cook over medium-to-high heat, stirring constantly, until thickened and bubbly. Stir in the salt, pepper, and 3 cups of the shredded cheese, stirring until the cheese is melted. Stir in the small-shell macaroni, the tomatoes, and the shredded chicken.

ASSEMBLY

Spray a 13 by 9-inch baking dish with nonstick cooking spray. Fill each jumbo shell carefully with the white cheddar macaroni and place each side-by-side in the dish. Sprinkle with the remaining 1 cup of cheese. Stir together the melted butter and the crushed cornflakes. Sprinkle evenly over the tops of the shells. Bake for 15 to 20 minutes, or until golden-brown on top.

Submitted by Lorie Roach
Macaroni and Cheese Recipe Contest, National Winner, 2007
Cook Off Location: Portland, OR

Tex-Mex Mac & Cheese

"The inspiration for this recipe actually came from a shopping trip to one of the many local farmers' markets here in Southern California. One lucky find was a box of "corn pasta." This recipe is equally fabulous with regular elbow macaroni, but I must give credit where credit is due. Viva la Cheese!"
—Suzy Weaver

Serves 8 or more

INGREDIENTS

8 ounces uncooked corn pasta large macaroni noodles (Found in most organic sections of the grocery store. If unable to find, use regular large elbow macaroni.)
4 quarts water
1 tablespoon salt

SAUCE
1/2 cup unsalted butter, plus extra for buttering baking dish
1 1/2 cups minced onion
1 tablespoon minced garlic
1 tablespoon freshly grated lime zest
1 tablespoon Worcestershire sauce
2 teaspoons chipotle-flavored hot sauce (or to taste)
1 teaspoon ground cumin
1/2 teaspoon celery salt
1/2 cup all-purpose flour
1 quart heavy cream
1 tablespoon dried Mexican oregano
2 tablespoons freshly minced cilantro, stems only
4 cups shredded Tillamook Mexican Blend with Pepper Jack and Medium Cheddar cheese

TOPPING
2 cups shredded Tillamook Mexican Blend with Monterey Jack and Medium Cheddar cheese
1/4 cup unsalted butter
1 teaspoon chili powder
1 cup panko bread crumbs
1/2 cup yellow cornmeal
1/2 cup chopped pepitas (pumpkin seeds)
Pinch of salt

GARNISH (optional)
1 cup Tillamook sour cream
2 teaspoons chopped cilantro leaves
1 tablespoon chopped green onions (light-green portion)
1/2 teaspoon freshly grated lime zest
Thinly sliced avocado

PREPARATION

Place the oven rack to the center of the oven and preheat the oven to 350°F. Butter a large ceramic or glass 10 by 20 by 2-inch-deep baking dish.

Melt the butter in a 4-quart, heavy-duty, nonstick pot over medium-low heat. Add the onion, garlic, and lime zest. Sweat over medium-low heat for 1 to 2 minutes, being careful not to brown the mixture. Add the Worcestershire and the hot sauce and cook for 30 seconds, scraping up any browned bits. Add the cumin and celery salt. Stir in the flour and cook over low heat for 3 to 4 minutes, stirring continuously.

Whisk in the cream until the mixture is smooth, and bring to a low simmer. Add the oregano and cilantro. Stirring frequently, continue to cook the sauce over low heat for 15 minutes. Reduce to three-fourths of its original volume. The sauce will thicken. Stir in the Mexican Blend until thoroughly melted.

Meanwhile, in a separate pot, bring 4 quarts of water and 1 tablespoon of salt to a boil. Cook the macaroni according to package directions (about 7 to 8 minutes), to the al dente stage. Drain and set aside, reserving 1/2 cup of the cooking water.

Carefully stir the cooked macaroni into the cheese sauce until it is well combined, adding the 1/2 cup of cooking water to thin the sauce a bit. Carefully pour the mixture into a prepared baking dish and lightly smooth the top.

TOPPING

Combine the butter and chili powder in a large microwave-safe dish. Melt the butter in the microwave on high for 30 seconds, or until melted. Stir in the bread crumbs, cornmeal, pepitas, and salt. Mix together with a fork until all the crumbs are moist.

Sprinkle a thick layer of the Mexican Blend with Monterey Jack and Medium Cheddar cheese evenly over the top of the dish. Top with the breadcrumb mixture. Bake, uncovered, for 30 to 45 minutes, until the cheese is bubbly and the top is a light golden-brown.

Blend the sour cream with the cilantro, green onions, and lime zest. Garnish each serving with a dollop of the flavored sour cream and avocado slices.

Submitted by Suzy Weaver
Macaroni and Cheese Recipe Contest, Regional Winner, 2006
Cook Off Location: Pasadena, CA

Mega-Cheesy Mac & Cheese
with Crab

"This is comfort-food gone upscale with the addition of the sweet, delicate crab. A great addition to an already yummy dish—the layers of cheese, macaroni, cream cheese, crab, and the crispy fried onion topping are an explosion of flavors in your mouth."
—Laura Najar

Makes 8 hearty servings

INGREDIENTS
1 pound elbow macaroni (or any shape)
5 tablespoons Tillamook butter
5 tablespoons all-purpose flour
2 1/2 cups whole milk
1/2 teaspoon salt
1/4 teaspoon freshly ground black
  pepper
1/4 teaspoon hot sauce
1/2 teaspoon minced garlic
1/4 teaspoon nutmeg
1/4 teaspoon seafood seasoning
2 1/2 cups freshly grated Parmesan
  cheese, divided
2 cups grated Tillamook Swiss cheese
2 cups grated Tillamook Monterey Jack
  cheese
8 ounces Havarti cheese, grated
4 ounces cream cheese, cubed to
  1/4-inch
12 ounces fresh cooked crab meat,
  picked clean
2/3 cup fresh or panko bread crumbs
1/8 cup freshly chopped parsley

PREPARATION
Preheat the oven to 350°F.

Bring 6 to 8 cups of water to a boil and cook pasta until very al dente (slightly undercooked). Do this step while the sauce is cooking below. Drain and return to the pot. If the pasta is done before the sauce, cover the pot and keep it warm.

Melt the butter over low heat in a medium saucepan. Add the flour, stirring to combine. Cook, stirring constantly, for 3 minutes. Increase the heat to medium, and slowly whisk in the milk to avoid lumps. Cook until thickened, about 4 to 5 minutes, stirring frequently. Remove from the heat, season with the salt, pepper, hot sauce, garlic, nutmeg, seafood seasoning, and 1 1/2 cups of grated Parmesan. Stir until the cheese is melted and the sauce is smooth. Add the sauce to the pasta and stir until well combined. Cover and set aside.

Combine 1 1/2 cups of Parmesan cheese in a large bowl, along with all the other grated cheeses. Toss to combine.

Place one-third of the macaroni and sauce in a 13 by 9-inch casserole dish. Top with one-third of the mixed cheeses, one-half of the cream cheese cubes, and one-half of the crab meat. Top with another one-third of macaroni, one-third of mixed cheese, the remaining cream cheese and crab. Top with last one-third of macaroni and the mixed cheeses, ending with a cheese layer.

Combine the bread crumbs and the parsley in a small bowl. Toss to combine. Sprinkle the topping evenly over the top of the macaroni and cheese.

Bake for 40 to 45 minutes, or until the macaroni and cheese is bubbly and hot and the top is golden-brown. Remove from the oven and allow to sit for 5 minutes before serving.

Submitted by Laura Najar
Macaroni and Cheese Recipe Contest, Regional Winner, 2006
Cook Off Location: San Francisco, CA

Mi Casa Chicken Pasta

"Mi Casa Chicken Pasta is a great one-dish meal that can be made ahead of time and then heated just before serving. The fajita-seasoned chicken adds a little South-of-the-Border flavor and gives the macaroni and cheese some added texture. This is one of those recipes that satisfies the moniker of 'comfort food,' and needs nothing more than a simple salad and some cornbread to make a complete dinner." —Terryl Propper

Serves 8 or more

INGREDIENTS

1 pound orecchiette pasta
5 tablespoons butter
1 large onion, finely diced
3/4 cup chopped multicolored bell peppers
4 large cloves garlic, run through a garlic press
4 tablespoons all-purpose flour
2 cups half-and-half
1 cup chicken stock
1 (4-ounce) can green chiles drained
2 cups shredded Tillamook Garlic Chili Pepper Cheddar
  cheese
2 cups shredded Tillamook Pepper Jack Cheddar cheese
2 cups shredded Tillamook Garlic White Cheddar cheese
2 1/2 cups shredded Tillamook Vintage White Extra Sharp
  Cheddar cheese
2 1/2 cups frozen Southwestern-flavored chicken strips,
  thawed
1 teaspoon salt
1 teaspoon freshly ground white pepper

TOPPING

1 cup shredded Tillamook Vintage White Extra Sharp
  Cheddar cheese
2 tablespoons melted butter
1 cup crushed multicolored tortilla chips

GARNISH

1 tablespoon freshly chopped fresh cilantro
1 sprig of cilantro
Mini hot red peppers

PREPARATION

Bring a pot of salted water to a boil over high heat. Add the pasta and cook for 10 to 12 minutes, to the al dente stage. Drain and set aside.

Preheat the oven to 400°F. Melt the butter in a large pot over medium heat and add the onion and bell pepper. Sauté for 2 to 3 minutes on medium heat until the onions are transparent. Add the garlic and continue to sauté for 2 minutes, stirring constantly. Add the flour and continue stirring for about 1 minute, being careful not to brown the mixture. Slowly add the half-and-half, stirring continuously after each addition, until the mixture begins to thicken. Add the chicken stock, a little at a time, and continue stirring until the mixture is thick enough to coat a wooden spoon. Add the green chiles. Remove from the heat and add the cheeses. Continue stirring until the cheese is melted. Add the chicken. Season to taste with salt and pepper. Pour the macaroni and cheese into a large casserole dish.

Spread 1 cup of the cheese over the top of the casserole. In a separate pot, melt 3 tablespoons of butter and combine with tortilla chips. Sprinkle of top of the casserole and bake for 20 minutes, or until it is hot and bubbly.

Garnish with the chopped cilantro. Decorate the plate with a sprig of cilantro and a mini hot red pepper.

Submitted by Terryl Propper
Macaroni and Cheese Recipe Contest, Regional Winner, 2007
Cook Off Location: Chicago, IL

Tillamook Three-Cheese Shells
with Prawns

This is an easy and delicious dish with a delightfully colorful presentation. For unique variations, you can always substitute other seafood choices.

Makes 10 individual servings

INGREDIENTS

1 pound medium prawns, peeled, deveined, cut lengthwise

1 1/4 cups shredded Tillamook Medium Cheddar cheese

1 1/4 cups shredded Tillamook Special Reserve Extra Sharp Cheddar cheese

1 1/4 cups shredded Tillamook Vintage White Medium Cheddar cheese

1 1/2 tablespoons olive oil

2 teaspoons dried basil or 2 tablespoons freshly chopped basil

1 3/4 teaspoons salt, divided

1/4 teaspoon freshly ground black pepper, plus an additional pinch

1 pound uncooked medium pasta shells

1 tablespoon salt

4 quarts of water

3 tablespoons Tillamook butter

2 tablespoons minced shallots

2 teaspoons minced garlic

1/4 cup dry vermouth

1 tablespoon tomato paste

3 tablespoons all-purpose flour

2 3/4 cups whole milk

3/4 cup whipping cream

1 teaspoon seafood base or 1/3 cup clam juice

20 tomato slices

1/3 cup freshly chopped parsley, for garnish

PREPARATION

Combine the cheese in a medium bowl and refrigerate. Toss the prawns in a small bowl with the oil, basil, 1/4 teaspoon of salt and the pepper. Reserve 2/3 cup of cheese for the topping. Cover and refrigerate.

Preheat the oven to 400°F. Lightly butter 10 (8-ounce) ramekins.

Bring the water and salt to a boil in a large pot, and add the pasta. Cook to the al dente stage. Drain the pasta in a colander and reserve.

Prepare the sauce while the pasta is cooking. Melt the butter in a 2-quart saucepan over medium heat. Add the shallots, and sauté until soft, about 3 minutes. Stir in the garlic, and cook for 1 minute. Pour in the vermouth and continue to cook over medium-high heat for 4 minutes. Stirring constantly, whisk in the flour, and continue to cook for 3 minutes. Add the tomato paste and whisk to combine. Over medium heat, gradually whisk in the milk and cream and cook, stirring constantly, until the sauce has thickened, about 4 to 5 minutes. Season with the seafood base or clam juice, the remaining 1 1/2 teaspoons of the salt, and a dash of pepper.
Add the bowl of mixed cheeses. Stir until the cheese is melted. Remove the pan from the heat and gently fold in the pasta.

Fill the prepared ramekins with the sauce and pasta mixture. Top each with equal amounts of tomato slices and prawn halves. Sprinkle with the reserved cheese. Place the ramekins on a baking sheet, and bake for 20 minutes, or until the cheese is bubbly and the prawns are cooked through. Allow to stand for 5 minutes before serving.

Garnish with the chopped parsley.

Mushroom Lover's Mac & Cheese

This earthy dish is a wonderful treat for the mushroom lover. We recommend a fresh green salad on the side.

Serves 10

INGREDIENTS

1/2 ounce dried porcini mushrooms

1/2 cup white wine

12 ounces dry whole-wheat penne pasta or regular penne pasta

6 tablespoons Tillamook unsalted butter, divided

2 tablespoons minced shallots

1 tablespoon minced garlic

1 teaspoon freshly minced thyme

1 teaspoon freshly minced sage

1 teaspoon freshly minced rosemary

12 ounces thinly sliced crimini or white mushrooms

4 tablespoons all-purpose flour

2 cups half-and-half

1/2 teaspoon freshly ground black pepper

3 1/2 cups shredded Tillamook Italian Blend with Mozzarella and Medium Cheddar cheese, divided

1/2 cup pine nuts, toasted

1/2 cup shredded Tillamook Vintage White Extra Sharp Cheddar cheese

1 1/2 tablespoons freshly chopped Italian parsley, for garnish

PREPARATION

Preheat the oven to 350°F. Lightly butter a 9 by 13-inch shallow baking dish.

Cover the dried porcini mushrooms in a small bowl with 1/2 cup of boiling water. Soak until softened, about 15 to 20 minutes. Pour into a strainer. Remove the mushrooms, squeezing the excess water back through the strainer. Reserve the liquid. Finely chop the mushrooms, and reserve.

Simmer the wine in a small saucepan or sauté pan, over medium heat, for 4 to 6 minutes, or until reduced by half. Reserve.

Bring 4 quarts of water to a boil. Add 1 tablespoon of salt and the pasta. Cook according to package directions, stirring occasionally, to the al dente stage. Drain the pasta in a colander and reserve.

Prepare the sauce while the pasta is cooking. Melt 4 tablespoons butter over medium heat in a large saucepan. Stir in the shallots, and cook for 2 minutes. Add the garlic, thyme, sage, and rosemary. Cook an additional minute. Stir in the porcini and crimini mushrooms, and 1/2 teaspoon of the salt. Cook, stirring frequently, until the mushrooms are browned and their cooking liquid has almost evaporated, about 8 to10 minutes.

Add the remaining butter, and melt. Add the flour, and cook, stirring constantly, for 3 minutes. Gradually add the half-and-half, and bring just to a boil, stirring constantly. Reduce the heat and simmer, stirring often, until the sauce thickens slightly, about 4 to 5 minutes.

Blend in the reserved mushroom liquid, the reduced wine, and the pepper. Add 3 cups of the Italian cheese, and stir until the cheese is melted. Remove the pan from the heat and gently fold in the pasta. Pour the mixture into a prepared baking dish. Top with the remaining 1/2 cup of Italian Blend and the Vintage White Extra Sharp Cheddar cheese, and the pine nuts.

Bake for 20 to 25 minutes, or until it is bubbly and the top begins to brown. Allow to stand for 5 minutes before serving. Garnish with the chopped parsley.

Autumn Comfort Mac

"Roasted butternut squash, fresh sage and pancetta are perfect companions in this warm, comforting dish. It's just right for autumn, when the weather is starting to turn cold and squash and sage are in season. The fall harvest butternut squash turns sweet and caramel after roasting, and is the perfect complement to the rich, creamy sauce."
—Veronica Vichit-Vadakan

Serves 8 or more

INGREDIENTS

1 butternut squash (approximately 2 pounds), peeled, cubed into 1-inch pieces
2 tablespoons olive oil
12 ounces cavatappi pasta (hollow corkscrew pasta)
3/4 cup shredded Tillamook Mozzarella cheese
3/4 cup shredded Tillamook Sharp Cheddar cheese
1/2 cup shredded Parmesan cheese
4 ounces dried pancetta
1 shallot, minced
4 tablespoons Tillamook unsalted butter
4 tablespoons all-purpose flour
2 cups whole milk
1/2 cup heavy cream or half-and-half
1 1/2 tablespoons freshly chopped sage
1 teaspoon freshly ground black pepper
4 ounces goat cheese, crumbled

TOPPING

1 tablespoon Tillamook unsalted sweet-cream butter
1 1/2 tablespoons freshly chopped sage
1/4 cup shredded Tillamook Mozzarella cheese
1/4 cup shredded Tillamook Sharp Cheddar cheese
2 tablespoons shredded Parmesan cheese
1 cup panko bread crumbs

PREPARATION

Preheat the oven to 450°F. Toss the butternut squash pieces with olive oil in a large bowl. Spread the squash pieces in a single layer on a cookie sheet. Bake for 20 minutes, stirring once. Remove when the squash is tender and caramel-brown. Set aside and reduce the oven to 350°F.

Bring 2 quarts of water to a boil. Add the pasta and cook approximately 8 minutes or to the al dente stage. Drain well.

Cook the pancetta over medium heat in a skillet for 6 minutes. Add the shallots, and cook for 2 minutes more. Remove from the heat.

Mix together the Mozzarella, Cheddar, and Parmesan cheese and set aside.

Melt the butter in a 2-quart sauce pan. Add the flour and, stirring constantly, cook for approximately 2 minutes, or until golden-brown. Add the milk and cream in a slow, steady stream, whisking constantly until smooth. Stir in 2 cups of the cheese mixture, and stir until the cheese is melted. Remove from the heat. Stir in the chopped sage. Season to taste with the pepper.

Fold the cooked pasta, cheese sauce, and pancetta mixture together in a large bowl. Gently fold in the squash and goat cheese. Pour into a lightly greased 9 by 13-inch baking pan.

To make the topping, melt 1 tablespoon butter in the microwave in a large glass bowl. Stir in the sage, the cheeses, and bread crumbs. Sprinkle over the top of the pasta mixture in the pan.

Bake at 350°F for 20 to 25 minutes, or until the cheese is bubbling.

Turn on the broiler and place the pan on the top rack of the oven. Brown for 3 minutes, or until golden-brown.

Remove from the oven and allow to rest for 10 minutes before serving. Sprinkle each serving with minced fresh sage, if desired.

Submitted by Veronica Vichit-Vadakan
Macaroni and Cheese Recipe Contest, Regional Winner, 2007
Cook Off Location: Portland, OR

Pepper Jack & Mac Roasted Rellenos

Wow your guests with this beautiful and creative dish. The pepper Jack cheese adds a surprising kick.

Serves 4

INGREDIENTS

8 poblano peppers, roasted, peeled, seeded
1 1/2 cups uncooked ditalini pasta
2 teaspoons salt, divided
2 1/2 tablespoons butter
2 1/2 tablespoons all-purpose flour
1 1/2 cups milk
1 1/2 cups shredded Tillamook Pepper Jack cheese
1/2 cup Tillamook sour cream
1 cup shredded Tillamook Colby Jack cheese
Tillamook sour cream, for garnish (optional)
1 large tomato, seeded, chopped (optional)

PREPARATION

Preheat the oven to 350°F.

To roast the peppers, place them on a hot grill or under a broiler until the skin is blackened and blistering, turning to ensure that all sides are roasted. Place the charred peppers in a plastic bag and steam until they are cool enough to handle. Carefully remove the skins. Cut a slit in the peppers and gently remove the seeds and veins (try to avoid tearing.) If desired, soak the peppers in cool, salted water for about an hour to decrease the heat of the peppers. Rinse, pat dry with paper towels, and reserve.

Bring 2 quarts of water to a boil in a large pot. Add the pasta and 1 teaspoon of the salt, and cook until the pasta is tender, about 8 minutes. Drain in colander and reserve.

Melt the butter over medium-high heat in a large, heavy saucepan or Dutch oven. Stir in the flour and 1 teaspoon of the salt and cook for 1 minute, stirring continuously. Gradually whisk in the milk, and stir until the sauce reaches a light boil, stirring constantly. Continue to cook until slightly thickened, about 2 minutes. Remove from the heat and add the pepper Jack cheese, stirring until fully melted. Stir in the sour cream and pasta, and mix until well combined.

Place the poblano peppers, open-side-up, in a baking pan that has been sprayed with nonstick cooking spray. Plump them out, so that they are full and open. Spoon the pasta-cheese mixture into the prepared peppers. Sprinkle the tops evenly with the Colby Jack cheese, and cover with aluminum foil.

Bake for 20 to 25 minutes, or until heated through and the cheese is melted.

Plate 2 peppers per serving. Top with a dollop of sour cream, and sprinkle with diced tomatoes as desired.

Submitted by Karen Gulkin
Macaroni and Cheese Recipe Contest, Regional Winner, 2005
Cook Off Location: Denver, CO

Tillamook Crab & Macaroni Bake

"A taste of my childhood, this deliciously light and fresh recipe brings back memories of trips to Tillamook and vacations to the beach. I hope that your family enjoys it as much as mine has over the years!" —Elizabeth Guise

Serves 8 or more

INGREDIENTS
10 ounces rotini pasta
3 slices white bread
2 tablespoons olive oil
1 3/4 teaspoon Old Bay® with Garlic and Herb seasoning, divided
3 tablespoons Tillamook butter
1/4 cup all-purpose flour
2 cups lowfat milk
1/2 teaspoon salt
1/4 teaspoon freshly ground black pepper
1/4 teaspoon granulated garlic
4 ounces cream cheese
1 cup grated Tillamook Medium Cheddar cheese
1 1/2 cups grated Tillamook Monterey Jack cheese
1/2 cup finely diced red bell pepper
2 tablespoon finely chopped yellow onion
1 tablespoon finely chopped shallots
3 tablespoons chopped cilantro
8 ounces fresh crabmeat

PREPARATION
Preheat the oven to 375°F.

Boil the pasta in salted water according to the package directions to the al dente stage. Drain, and reserve.

Place the slices of bread on a baking sheet. Drizzle with oil, sprinkle with 3/4 teaspoon of the Old Bay seasoning, and bake for 5 to 7 minutes until golden brown. Turn, and bake an additional 5 minutes until golden. Remove from oven and allow to cool.

Grate the cooled bread slices, and reserve.

Melt the butter over medium heat in a large saucepan. Add the flour and whisk until smooth. Continue stirring the butter and flour mixture over medium heat for 2 to 3 minutes until it has a slightly nutty aroma. Pour in the milk while whisking and whisk until smooth. Cook, while stirring constantly, for 2 to 3 minutes until the mixture thickens. Add salt, pepper, granulated garlic, and the remaining Old Bay seasoning. Add the cream cheese and whisk until smooth.

Remove from heat and add the grated Cheddar and Monterey Jack cheese. Stir with a wooden spoon until smooth. Stir in the peppers, onions, shallots, and cilantro. Stir in the pasta, and gently fold in the crab meat. Spray a large shallow (12 by 1 1/2-inch) ceramic casserole dish with pan spray. Pour in filling and spread out evenly.

Bake for 15 to 20 minutes, or until golden-brown and bubbling around the edge.

Submitted by Elizabeth Guise
Macaroni and Cheese Recipe Contest, National Winner, 2006
Cook Off Location: Tillamook, OR

Prosciutto Mushroom
Macaroni & Cheese

Add some interest with earthy mushrooms and delicate, salty prosciutto.

Serves 4

INGREDIENTS
1 1/2 cups uncooked elbow macaroni
2 tablespoons all-purpose flour
1/2 teaspoon dry mustard
1/4 teaspoon paprika
1/4 teaspoon freshly ground black
   pepper
1 3/4 cups whole milk
1 cup shredded Tillamook Medium
   Cheddar cheese
1 1/2 cups shredded Tillamook Colby
   Jack cheese

TOPPING
1/4 cup plus 2 tablespoons Tillamook
   butter, divided
1/2 cup finely chopped Portobello
   mushrooms
1/4 cup freshly chopped green onions
1 teaspoon freshly minced garlic
1 cup dry bread crumbs
1/2 cup coarsely chopped prosciutto
1/2 cup shredded Tillamook Monterey
   Jack cheese

PREPARATION
Preheat the oven to 400°F.

Bring 2 quarts of salted water to a boil in a large pot. Add the macaroni, and return to a boil. Reduce the heat. Cook for 7 to 9 minutes, or to the al dente stage. Drain, rinse with cold water, and drain again. Cover and reserve.

Melt 2 tablespoons of the butter in a large saucepan over medium heat. Add the flour, mustard, paprika, and pepper. Stir until well mixed. Cook for 2 minutes. Add the milk, and whisk until smooth. Cook for 2 to 4 minutes, until thickened and bubbly, stirring constantly. Remove from the heat and slowly add the Cheddar and Colby Jack cheeses, stirring constantly, until all are melted together. Mix the cheese sauce with the macaroni in a large pot. Cover and reserve.

For the topping, melt the butter in a 12-inch sauté pan over medium-high heat. Add the mushrooms, green onions, and garlic. Sauté until the mushrooms start to brown, about 4 to 6 minutes. Place the onion and mushroom mixture into a 2-quart mixing bowl. Add the bread crumbs, and mix thoroughly. Add the prosciutto and the Jack cheese, and mix again. Drizzle the bread-crumb mixture with 1/4 cup of melted butter and stir until well combined.

In four-single serving prepared casserole dishes, or (20-ounce) au gratin dishes, add one quarter of the macaroni and cheese to each. With the back of a large spoon, press the macaroni and cheese down, forming a bowl-shaped hollow. Fill each hollow with one quarter of the crumb topping. Level the tops, pressing firmly.

Place all four on a baking sheet and bake for 20 minutes.

Submitted by Mike Rhineheart
Macaroni and Cheese Recipe Contest, Regional Winner, 2005
Cook Off Location: San Jose, CA

Roasted Peppers, Chicken & Cheese

A crowd favorite, this dish is perfect for parents and kids alike.

Serves 8 to 10

INGREDIENTS

2 cups shredded Tillamook Vintage White Extra Sharp Cheddar cheese, divided

1 1/2 cups coarse, fresh bread crumbs

2 tablespoons shredded Parmesan cheese

1 teaspoon paprika

8 tablespoons Tillamook unsalted butter, divided

1 tablespoon olive oil

4 to 5 thinly sliced scallions or green onions

1 teaspoon chili powder

1 teaspoon oregano

2 teaspoons freshly minced garlic

1 tablespoon plus 1/2 teaspoon salt, divided

1/4 teaspoon freshly ground black pepper

5 to 6 medium-large fresh pasilla or poblano peppers, roasted, with membranes removed, and diced to 1/2-inch

4 cups (1 pound) cooked shredded chicken, light and dark meat

1 pound uncooked dry farfalle (bow-tie) pasta

3 tablespoons all-purpose flour

3 cups whole milk

1 1/2 cups shredded Tillamook Pepper Jack cheese

PREPARATION

Preheat the oven to 350°F.

Lightly butter a 4-quart shallow baking dish.

To make the topping, combine 1/2 cup of the Cheddar, the bread crumbs, Parmesan, and paprika in a small bowl. Melt 4 tablespoons of the butter. Toss the breadcrumbs with the melted butter and reserve.

Melt 1 tablespoon of butter with the olive oil, over medium heat, in a large sauté pan. Stir in the scallions, chili powder, oregano, garlic, 1 tablespoon of the salt, pepper, and diced peppers. Cook for 3 minutes, stirring frequently. Reduce the heat to low. Gently stir in the chicken and cook for about 2 minutes, until heated through. Remove from the heat and transfer to a large bowl. Reserve.

Bring 4 quarts of water to a boil. Add 1/2 teaspoon of the salt and pasta. Cook according to package directions, stirring occasionally, to the al dente stage. Drain the pasta in a colander and fold it into the chicken mixture.

Prepare the sauce while the pasta is cooking. Melt the remaining butter over medium heat in a large saucepan. Whisk in the flour and cook for 3 minutes, whisking constantly. Gradually add the milk and bring just to a boil, whisking constantly. Reduce the heat and simmer, stirring often, until the sauce begins to thicken, about 4 to 5 minutes. Add the pepper Jack and the remaining Cheddar. Stir, until the cheese is melted. Remove from the heat. Gently fold the sauce into the chicken/pasta mixture.

Spread the mixture evenly in a prepared baking dish. Top with the reserved bread crumb mixture. Bake for 20 to 25 minutes or until bubbly, and the top begins to brown. Allow to stand for 5 minutes before serving.

The Ultimate Comfort Food
Macaroni & Cheese

"Macaroni and Cheese has been a staple on the dinner table for decades! The creative blend of cheeses in this comfort food is so smooth and delicious that any cheese lover will find it irresistible. This recipe brings back wonderful memories of Mom's home cooking." —Cheryl Hart

Serves 8 to 10 as a main course

INGREDIENTS

8 tablespoons (1 stick) unsalted Tillamook butter, divided
1 1/2 teaspoons garlic powder, divided
3 cups (about 1/2 loaf) good white crusty bread, cut into 1/4- to 1/2-inch pieces
2 cups shredded Tillamook Vintage White Extra Sharp Cheddar cheese, divided
1/2 cup shredded Swiss cheese
1 1/4 cups shredded Romano cheese
2 teaspoons salt, divided
1 pound large uncooked rigatoni pasta
1/4 cup all-purpose flour
2 1/2 cups half-and-half (1 quart), room temperature
2 cups whole milk
1/2 teaspoon freshly ground black pepper
1/2 to 1 teaspoon ground or whole red pepper flakes
1/4 teaspoon nutmeg
2 cups shredded Tillamook Sharp Cheddar cheese
1 1/2 tablespoons freshly chopped parsley

PREPARATION

Preheat the oven to 350°F.

Butter and set aside a 9 by 13-inch casserole dish. To make the topping, melt 4 tablespoons of butter with 1/2 teaspoon of the garlic powder. Place the bread cubes in a medium bowl. Toss the melted garlic butter with the bread cubes and reserve.

Combine 1 cup of the Vintage White, 1/2 cup of the Swiss, and 1/4 of the Romano in a separate small bowl. Reserve for the topping.

Bring 6 quarts of water to a boil in a large pot. Add 1 1/2 tablespoons of salt and the pasta. Cook, according to package directions, to the al dente stage. Drain in a colander and reserve.

Prepare the sauce while the pasta is cooking. Melt 4 tablespoons of butter in a large saucepan over medium heat. Whisk in the flour and cook for 3 minutes, whisking constantly. Gradually add the half-and-half and milk, and bring just to a boil, whisking constantly. Reduce the heat and simmer, whisking often, until the sauce slightly thickens, about 4 to 5 minutes.

Stir in the remaining garlic powder, salt, pepper, pepper flakes, and nutmeg. Add the remaining Vintage White, Swiss, Romano, and Sharp cheeses, stirring until the cheese is melted. Remove the pan from the heat. Fold the pasta into the cheese sauce.

Pour the mixture into a prepared baking dish. Sprinkle with the reserved cheese. Top with the bread-cube mixture. Bake for 25 to 30 minutes, or until the cheese is bubbly and the top begins to brown. Allow to stand for 5 minutes before serving. Garnish with the chopped parsley.

Submitted by Cheryl Hart
Macaroni and Cheese Recipe Contest, Regional Winner, 2005
Cook Off Location: Phoenix, AZ

LEFT TO RIGHT:

Leslie, Derrick,
Don, Desi,
Julie (sitting),
Bryson (in Julie's lap)

Main Course

Don and Desi Josi
Wilsonview Diary, Inc.

We take pride in what we do and the product we produce."

Wilsonview Dairy was established in 1918 by Alfred Josi, a Swiss emigrant. His wife, Cecilia, also came from a dairy family, whose heritage included the head buttermaker at the Nehalem, Oregon creamery.

In those days, the cows were milked by hand, with each family member taking special responsibility for one individual animal.

Today, the dairy has grown from the original sixty acres to 250, with Alfred's grandson, Don, his wife Desi and their son Derrick managing the day-to-day operations. Don says, "dairying is in my blood." He has followed in his grandfather's footsteps by serving as a board member of the Tillamook County Creamery Association.

Cheesy Chicken Penne

Be creative with the mushroom choice—a mixture of varying types adds a whole new dimension.

Serves 8 to 10

INGREDIENTS

1/4 cup Tillamook unsalted butter, plus additional for preparing the baking dish
3/4 pound fresh mushrooms, sliced
2 cloves garlic, minced
1/2 teaspoon salt, divided
1/4 teaspoon freshly ground black pepper, divided
1/4 cup all-purpose flour
2 cups chicken broth
1 cup half-and-half, or whole milk
4 cups shredded Tillamook Sharp Cheddar cheese, divided
3 tablespoons dry sherry
1/2 pound penne pasta, cooked, drained
4 cups pulled, cooked chicken (2 whole roasted chickens)
1 1/2 cups toasted fresh bread crumbs

PREPARATION

Preheat the oven to 350°F. Butter a shallow 3-quart baking dish and set aside.

Melt 1/4 cup of the butter in a large, heavy-bottomed saucepan over medium-high heat. Add the mushrooms and garlic and sprinkle with 1/4 teaspoon of the salt, and 1/8 teaspoon of the pepper. Sauté until the liquid released from the mushrooms has evaporated, about 12 minutes. Reduce the heat to medium.

Sprinkle the flour evenly over the mushrooms, and cook, stirring constantly, for one minute. Gradually add the broth and half-and-half, stirring until no lumps of flour remain. Bring to a simmer, stirring frequently, reduce the heat. Simmer until the sauce has thickened, about 3 to 5 minutes. Remove from the heat and add 3 cups of the cheese, and the sherry, stirring constantly until the cheese melts. Stir in the remaining salt and pepper.

Stir the pasta and chicken into the cheese sauce. Mix the remaining cheese and the bread crumbs and sprinkle evenly over the top of the casserole. Bake, uncovered, until the sauce is bubbling and the top is lightly browned, about 35 to 40 minutes.

Baked Orzo
with Shrimp & Lemon

Flavors of the Mediterranean blend nicely in this simple baked dish.

Serves 8

INGREDIENTS

1 pound medium shrimp,
  peeled, deveined
1 (1-pound) package orzo
Zest of 2 lemons
1/4 cup freshly chopped parsley
3 tablespoons olive oil
1 cup chopped onion
2 teaspoons minced garlic
2 teaspoons dried oregano
1/8 teaspoon red chili flakes
1 (14.5-ounce) can diced
  tomatoes
1/8 teaspoon salt
1 cup crumbled feta cheese
1 1/2 cups shredded Tillamook
  Mozzarella cheese

PREPARATION

Preheat the oven to 400°F.

Cook and drain the orzo according to package directions, reserving 1 1/2 cups of the cooking liquid. Combine the zest and parsley in a small bowl, reserving 1 tablespoon for the garnish.

Heat the oil in a large skillet over medium-high heat. Add the onion, and cook until soft. Add the garlic, oregano, and chili flakes. Cook for 2 minutes. Stir in the tomatoes and salt, and cook for 2 minutes. Add the shrimp and cook until just pink.

Combine the orzo, tomato-shrimp mixture, feta, parsley mixture, and reserved liquid in a large bowl. Spread evenly in a greased 9 by 13-inch baking dish, and top with the cheese. Bake for 20 to 25 minutes until bubbly and browned. Garnish with the reserved parsley-lemon mixture.

Know the Terminology!

Turophobia : The fear of cheese.

Cheesemonger : A person who sells cheese. A monger is a broker or dealer. The word monger is usually used in combination with another word, such as in alemonger.

Turophile : A lover of cheese. It comes from the Greek words for cheese (tyros) and lover (philos).

Shrimp & Tillamook Cheese Linguine

Simple, but bursting with flavor.

Serves 4

INGREDIENTS

1 pound medium shrimp, shelled, deveined
8 ounces dry linguine
1/8 cup olive oil, divided
1 tablespoon minced shallots
1 cup cream or half-and-half
1 1/4 cups shredded Tillamook Fancy Medium Cheddar cheese
Salt
Freshly ground black pepper
1 ounce sherry
1 tablespoon dijon mustard

PREPARATION

Cook the linguine in a large pot of boiling salted water until just tender. Meanwhile, heat a sauté pan with 1/2 of the oil. Add the shallots and cook for one minute over medium heat. Add the cream and bring to a boil. When the cream is just beginning to boil, add the cheese, a little bit at a time. Stir constantly, until all the cheese is melted. Reduce the heat to low and let simmer. Season to taste with salt and pepper.

Place the remaining oil in a sauté pan and heat. Add the shrimp. When hot, add the sherry and mustard. Place the linguine into a bowl and mix with the cheese sauce. Place onto serving plates and top with the shrimp mixture.

Serve immediately.

Created by Marcel Lasheme, Executive Regional Chef
Jake's Famous Crawfish Restaurant
Portland, Oregon

Grilled Chicken Breast Stuffed with
Mushrooms, Spinach & Tillamook Sharp Cheddar Cheese

A creative way to add a little flair to simple chicken. Be creative and add other vegetables as you wish!

Serves 4

INGREDIENTS

4 (6-ounce) boneless, skinless chicken breasts
3 tablespoons olive oil, divided
1/2 medium onion, diced
1 cup small crimini mushrooms, sliced
Salt
Freshly ground black pepper
2 cloves garlic, minced
4 ounces frozen chopped spinach, thawed and squeezed dry
Pinch of ground nutmeg
2 cups grated Tillamook Sharp Cheddar cheese

PREPARATION

Heat a medium-sized sauté pan over medium-high heat. Add the olive oil and sauté the onions until they wilt, about 5 minutes. Add the mushrooms and season with salt and pepper. Sauté for an additional 7 minutes. Add the garlic and cook for 3 minutes. Remove from the heat and cool to room temperature. Stir in the drained spinach and nutmeg. Add the cheese and stir to combine.

Preheat the grill to medium-high.

On a cutting board, slice a pocket, about 1-inch deep, along the length of each breast. Stuff each breast evenly with the mushroom, spinach, and cheese mixture, and secure with a toothpick. Season with salt and pepper.

Lightly brush the grill rack with the remaining oil. Grill the chicken breasts for about 6 minutes, turn, and cook an additional 6 minutes. The chicken is done when an instant-read thermometer inserted into the thickest part of the breast registers 165°F.

Serve with couscous, rice, or a salad of baby greens with vinaigrette dressing.

Cheesy Baked Ziti

Easy and cheesy—a perfect Italian dinner.

Serves 6

INGREDIENTS

1 (16-ounce) package of ziti or other tube-shaped pasta
6 to 8 quarts water
1 tablespoon Tillamook butter
1 1/2 cups heavy cream
1/4 teaspoon ground nutmeg
1/3 cup grated Parmesan cheese, plus extra to spread on top
1 tablespoon olive oil
1 (22-ounce) jar prepared marinara sauce
2 cups shredded Tillamook Mozzarella cheese
1/2 cup bread crumbs
Salt
Freshly ground black pepper

PREPARATION

Preheat the oven to 375°F.

Boil the pasta in the water until it has reached the al dente stage. Drain and reserve.

Heat the butter and heavy cream over medium-high heat in a 1 to 2 quart saucepan, stirring frequently. When the mixture starts to bubble, stir in the nutmeg and Parmesan. Season with salt and pepper. Reduce the heat to medium, and cook for 3 minutes more, stirring frequently.

Grease a large 13 by 9 by 2-inch baking dish with the olive oil. Pour the pasta into the baking dish. Add the marinara sauce, cream sauce, and mozzarella to the pasta, and stir well.

Sprinkle the top with the bread crumbs and Parmesan. Bake for 25 minutes, or until bubbling. Bake an additional 5 minutes, or place under the broiler for 5 minutes to crisp the top, if needed.

Tillamook Cheese Manicotti

Quick and easy, and sure to please even the pickiest palate.

Serves 4 to 6

INGREDIENTS

12 dry manicotti shells
3/4 cup shredded Tillamook Mozzarella cheese
3/4 cup shredded Tillamook Sharp Cheddar cheese
1/2 cup shredded Parmesan cheese
1 (24-ounce) jar of prepared marinara sauce
1 pound ricotta cheese
2 large eggs, lightly beaten
2 tablespoons freshly minced Italian parsley
Salt
Freshly ground black pepper
2 tablespoons olive oil

PREPARATION

Preheat the oven to 375°F.

Bring a large pot of water to boil over high heat. Cook the manicotti shells to the al dente stage. Drain and pat dry. Combine the Mozzarella, Cheddar, and Parmesan in a bowl. Cover the bottom of a 9 by 13-inch baking dish with 1 cup of the marinara sauce. Combine the ricotta, 1/2 of the cheese mixture, and the eggs in a mixing bowl. Season to taste with the parsley, salt, and pepper.

Spoon the cheese mixture into the manicotti shells and align them side-by-side in the baking dish. Cover the filled manicotti with the remaining sauce and drizzle the olive oil over the shells. Scatter the remaining cheese on top, and bake for 25 minutes.

Green Chile Enchiladas

Traditional Mexican flavor—get creative and adjust the spiciness to your own preference.

Serves 4 to 6

INGREDIENTS
1 large can whole tomatoes
1 large yellow onion, diced
5 tablespoons chili powder
Pinch of cumin
Salt
Freshly ground black pepper
1 small pinch of cinnamon
1 teaspoon of sugar (optional)
1 1/4 cups vegetable oil
1 dozen super-size white or yellow corn
   tortillas
4 cups shredded Tillamook Medium
   Cheddar cheese
4 cups shredded Tillamook Monterey
   Jack cheese
2 large cans whole green chiles
Olives, for garnish

PREPARATION
Preheat the oven to 325°F.

Prepare a 9 by 13-inch baking pan by lightly greasing it with vegetable oil. Combine in a 6 quart pot: the tomatoes, onion, chili powder, cumin, salt, pepper, cinnamon, and sugar (optional to taste). Bring to a boil. Cover, reduce the heat, and simmer for 15 minutes. Lightly pan-fry the tortillas in vegetable oil.

Blend the cheese together in a bowl. Dip the tortillas individually into the sauce and reserve, laying flat on a plate. Stuff and roll each tortilla with the cheeses and green chile. (You will have cheese left over, set this aside for later use.) Place the enchiladas in a row in a 9 by 13-inch baking pan. Pour the sauce over the enchiladas. Top with the remaining cheeses. Bake for 25 minutes. Serve individually with a dollop of sour cream and an olive on top.

Submitted by Michelle Lisa Goodwin
Tillamook Cheese Recipe Contest 2001
Napa, CA

Twice-Baked Cheese Soufflé
with Deviled Crab Sauce

An elegant entrée.

Serves 4

INGREDIENTS
4 tablespoons Tillamook butter, divided
1/4 cup grated Parmesan cheese
1/4 cup all-purpose flour
1 cup milk, heated
1 cup shredded Tillamook Sharp Cheddar cheese
1/4 teaspoon nutmeg
3 large eggs, separated
Deviled Crab Sauce (recipe follows)

DEVILED CRAB SAUCE
2 tablespoons minced shallots
1 tablespoon minced celery
1 tablespoon Tillamook butter
1 tablespoon flour
1 1/4 cups whole milk
1 1/2 teaspoons Dijon mustard
1/4 teaspoon Tabasco® pepper sauce
Pinch of salt
1 tablespoon chopped chives
4 ounces fresh crab meat
Freshly ground black pepper

PREPARATION
Preheat the oven to 350°F.

Using 1 tablespoon of butter, coat the bottom and sides of 4 (8-ounce) ramekins. Sprinkle each ramekin with 1 tablespoon of Parmesan cheese.

Melt 3 tablespoons of the butter over medium heat in a medium saucepan. Add the flour and stir constantly for about 4 minutes, or until the butter has a nutty aroma, being careful not to let it brown. Slowly add the milk, stirring for about 3 to 4 minutes, until the mixture has thickened. Stir in the cheese and nutmeg. Remove from the heat, and allow to cool slightly, about 10 minutes. Slowly whisk in the egg yolks.

Place the egg whites in a medium bowl and beat them until they form stiff peaks. Gently fold the whites into the cheese mixture.

Spoon the soufflé mixture into the prepared ramekins. Place the ramekins in a 10-inch square baking pan, set on the middle oven rack and pour boiling water into the pan, about two-thirds the way up the sides of the ramekins. Bake for about 20 minutes until the soufflés have risen, the egg appears set, and the tops are golden-brown. Remove and allow to cool. (The tops will collapse.) Soufflés can be set aside for an hour until ready to serve.

Preheat the oven to 425°F.

Prepare the Deviled Crab Sauce. Place the soufflés on a baking sheet and bake for 8 to 10 minutes until puffed. Serve immediately with Deviled Crab Sauce.

PREPARING THE DEVILED CRAB SAUCE
Sauté the shallots and celery in butter in a small saucepan until tender. Add the flour and stir over low heat for 1 to 2 minutes. Stir in the milk, mustard, pepper sauce, salt, and pepper. Simmer for about 10 minutes, stirring constantly, until smooth. Gently stir in the chives and crab. Season to taste with salt and pepper. Cover and keep warm until ready to use.

CHEF'S NOTE
To make a day ahead: Allow the soufflés to cool, then cover and refrigerate overnight. Remove from the refrigerator 1/2 hour before reheating.

Shredded Pork Enchiladas

A twist on a traditional Mexican dish. Making the sauce adds your own personal flair.

Serves 6

INGREDIENTS

1 1/2 pounds pork shoulder, cubed to 1-inch
2/3 cup chopped onion
1 teaspoon salt
1/4 teaspoon freshly ground black pepper
1 cup shredded Tillamook Monterey Jack cheese
1 cup shredded Tillamook Medium Cheddar cheese
3 1/2 cups enchilada sauce, divided (recipe follows)
12 (6-inch) corn tortillas
2 tablespoons vegetable oil

ENCHILADA SAUCE

2 tablespoons vegetable oil
3 cloves garlic, minced
2 tablespoons chili powder
1 (28-ounce) can diced tomatoes
1/2 canned chipotle chiles en adobo, or more to taste
1 tablespoon all-purpose flour
1 cup chicken broth

PREPARATION

Add 1 quart of water to a 4-quart saucepan and bring to a boil. Stir in the pork, onion, salt, and pepper, and simmer for 45 minutes until the pork is tender. Strain and set aside to cool.

Preheat the oven to 350°F. Combine the cheeses in a small bowl and set aside. Shred the pork into a medium bowl and combine with 1/2 cup of the enchilada sauce.

Brush both sides of the tortillas lightly with oil. Working in batches, stack the tortillas 2-high on a baking sheet. Heat in the oven for 3 minutes, just until tortillas are warm and pliable. Remove the tortillas from the oven. Make a single stack, cover with a kitchen towel, and keep warm.

PREPARING THE ENCHILADA SAUCE

Heat the oil over low heat in a 2-quart saucepan. Add the garlic and chili powder and sauté for 1 minute. Purée the tomatoes, chilis, flour, and garlic mixture until smooth. Pour the purée back into the pan and simmer for 10 minutes, stirring occasionally. Add the broth, and continue to simmer for 30 minutes more, stirring occasionally.

ASSEMBLY

Spread 3/4 cup of enchilada sauce on the bottom of a lightly greased 9 by 13-inch baking dish. Lay a warm tortilla on your clean work surface. Sprinkle a scant tablespoon of cheese and top with a scant 1/4 cup of pork filling across the middle of each tortilla. Roll the tortillas, and place seam-side down in the baking dish. Completely cover the enchiladas with the remaining sauce. Sprinkle with the remaining cheese. Bake until the cheese is melted and the sauce is bubbling, about 20 to 25 minutes. Allow to cool 10 minutes and serve.

Polenta & Roasted Vegetable "Lasagna"

A twist on traditional lasagna, using the nutty flavor of polenta and a mixture of vegetables.

Makes 8 to 10 servings

INGREDIENTS

4 cups cold water
1 1/2 cups yellow cornmeal
1 1/4 teaspoons salt
1 (2-pound) package (8 cups) shredded
  Tillamook Mozzarella cheese
2 large eggs
2 red bell peppers, julienne
2 medium zucchinis, sliced
1 medium eggplant, cubed
1/2 pound mushrooms, quartered
2 tablespoons olive oil
Salt
Freshly ground black pepper
1 (12-ounce) jar prepared marinara
  sauce

PREPARATION

Preheat the oven to 375°F.

Boil 2 1/2 cups of cold water in a medium saucepan. Whisk together the remaining 1 1/2 cups of cold water with the cornmeal and the salt. Add the cornmeal mixture to the boiling water, whisking constantly. Cook, and stir until the mixture boils. Reduce the heat to low. Cook until very thick, stirring occasionally, for 10 minutes. Remove from the heat and stir in the cheese. Allow to cool completely. Whisk in the eggs.

Toss the bell peppers, zucchini, eggplant, and mushrooms with olive oil, in a large roasting pan. Roast until tender, stirring once, for 30 minutes. Remove from the oven and season with salt and pepper.

Spread the cornmeal mixture evenly into a greased 9 by 13-inch baking dish and bake for 20 minutes. Remove from the oven.

Spread half of the marinara sauce on top. Spoon half of the vegetables on top of the sauce, and sprinkle with half of the cheese. Repeat the layers with the second half of the sauce, vegetables, and cheese.

Bake until golden-brown, about 25 minutes. Allow to cool for 10 minutes before cutting.

Creamy Tillamook
Cheese & Seafood Enchiladas

Cheesy goodness with the flavors of the ocean.

Makes 6 servings

INGREDIENTS

8 ounces cream cheese, softened
1/2 cup shredded Tillamook Pepper Jack cheese, divided
2 tablespoons white cooking wine
6 ounces frozen shrimp, roughly chopped
6 ounces crab meat, picked clean and roughly chopped
4 tablespoons vegetable oil
12 white or yellow corn tortillas
3/4 cup finely sliced scallions
3 cloves garlic, minced
3 tablespoons Tillamook butter
1 tablespoon all-purpose flour
1 teaspoon salt
1/2 teaspoon freshly ground black pepper
2 1/2 cups heavy cream or half-and-half
1 teaspoon finely chopped cilantro
1 tablespoon finely chopped oregano
1 cup shredded Tillamook Pepper Jack cheese
1/2 teaspoon ground paprika
1/2 teaspoon ground cayenne pepper

PREPARATION

Preheat the oven to 350°F. Put the cream cheese in a mixing bowl with a paddle attachment and add 1/2 cup of the cheese and wine. Beat on low speed until almost smooth. Stir in the shrimp and crab. Store the mixture in the refrigerator.

Heat the vegetable oil in a saucepan over medium heat for 1 minute. Dip the tortillas, one at a time, in the hot oil until they become limp. Drain on paper towels. Spoon about 1/4 cup of the seafood filling onto each tortilla and roll them tightly. Place the enchiladas side-by-side, seam-side down, in a casserole baking dish. Reserve.

In a medium saucepan, cook 1/3 cup of the scallions and garlic in the butter over low heat for 2 to 3 minutes. Stir in the flour, salt, pepper, cream, cilantro, and oregano. Bring to a low simmer for 1 to 2 minutes. Pour this sauce over the enchiladas.

Cover and bake for 15 minutes. Remove the cover and sprinkle the remaining cheese over the top of the enchiladas. Bake for an additional 5 to 10 minutes, or until the cheese bubbles. Remove the enchiladas from the oven and evenly sprinkle the remaining scallions, paprika, and cayenne over the top. Serve immediately.

Roasted Salmon
with Cheddar Dijon Béchamel

Simple yet elegant, enjoy the flavors of the Northwest and France.

Makes 6 servings

INGREDIENTS

6 (6-ounce) center-cut salmon fillets, skin-on (1 1/2 to 2 pounds sea bass or red snapper fillets may be substituted for salmon.)
3 tablespoons extra virgin olive oil
1 tablespoon Dijon mustard
Freshly ground black pepper
1 1/2 cups whole milk, or half-and-half
1/4 cup Dijon mustard
1 tablespoon all-purpose flour
1 large egg yolk
2 1/4 cups shredded Tillamook Vintage White Extra Sharp Cheddar cheese, divided
Salt
3 cups hot, cooked wild rice or brown rice

PREPARATION

Position the oven rack in the upper third of the oven and preheat to 425°F. Line a baking sheet with aluminum foil.

Place the fillets, skin-sides down, on a baking sheet. Mix the olive oil and mustard, and brush on the tops and sides of the salmon and sprinkle with pepper. Roast until the fish is just opaque, about 10 to 12 minutes.

Meanwhile, prepare the sauce by combining the milk, mustard, flour, and egg yolk in a small saucepan. Whisk to blend, and cook over medium heat, whisking gently and constantly, until the mixture just begins to bubble, about 10 to 15 minutes. Remove from the heat and add 3/4 cup of the cheese. Stir, until the cheese melts. Season with salt and pepper.

To serve, place a spoonful of wild rice on serving plates. Lift the fillets from the skin with a metal spatula, and place the salmon on the rice. Spoon the sauce over the fish and the wild rice. Sprinkle each serving with 1/4 cup of the remaining cheese.

The Birth of Cheese?

No one really knows who made the first cheese. According to an ancient legend, it was made accidentally by an Arabian merchant who put his supply of milk into a pouch made from a sheep's stomach, as he set out on a day's journey across the desert. The rennet in the lining of the pouch, combined with the heat of the sun, caused the milk to separate into curd and whey. That night he found that they whey satisfied his thirst, and the cheese (curd) had a delightful flavor which satisfied his hunger.

Savory Tomato Tart
with Pesto & Cheesy Custard

Serve with a large tossed salad topped with more fresh tomatoes.

Serves 6

INGREDIENTS
1 unbaked prepared pie crust
3 large eggs
1/3 cup cream
1/4 cup shredded Parmesan cheese
1 teaspoon salt
1/8 teaspoon freshly ground black
   pepper
1/4 cup prepared pesto
1 cup shredded Tillamook
   Mozzarella cheese
7 Roma tomatoes, cored and cut into
   1/4-inch slices

PREPARATION
Preheat the oven to 400°F.

Line a 9-inch tart pan with the dough and cut away the excess from the sides. Chill for 30 minutes.

With a fork, prick the bottom of the pie shell. Bake for 10 minutes until the crust is light golden-brown. Allow to cool.

Reduce the oven temperature to 375°F

In a medium bowl with a pour spout, whisk together the eggs, cream, Parmesan, salt, and pepper. Reserve.

Spread the pesto over the bottom of the crust, and sprinkle with the cheese. Working from the outside in, overlap the tomato slices in concentric circles, covering the crust completely. Pour the custard over the tomatoes.

Bake for 35 to 45 minutes, or until the custard is set. Allow to sit for 15 minutes before serving.

Chicken Pot Pie
with Tillamook Extra Sharp Cheddar & Green Onion Biscuit Crust

Classic comfort food—just a little better with sharp cheddar.

Serves 4

BATTER
1 1/2 cups all-purpose flour
1/2 tablespoon baking soda
1/2 teaspoon salt
4 tablespoons Tillamook butter
1 cup buttermilk
1/4 cup chopped green onion
1 1/2 cups shredded Tillamook Vintage White Extra Sharp White Cheddar cheese

FILLING (dice and blanch or sauté in advance)
2 cups diced cooked chicken
1/2 cup diced onion
1/2 cup diced carrot
1/2 cup diced celery
1/2 cup diced potatoes
3 cups hot, cooked wild rice or brown rice
1/2 cup frozen or fresh peas
3 tablespoons butter
3 tablespoons all-purpose flour
3 cups chicken stock or bouillon
1 tablespoon thyme
1/2 tablespoon freshly ground black pepper
1 teaspoon salt
2 tablespoons freshly chopped parsley

PREPARATION
Preheat the oven to 375°F.

Combine the flour, baking soda, and salt in a medium mixing bowl. Cut the butter into the flour mixture until it is crumbly and resembles coarse meal. Blend in the buttermilk, onion, and cheese. This batter will be loose, like spoon biscuits or shortcake. Reserve.

Combine the chicken and vegetables. These may be cooked by any method you like. Just make sure they are cooked through, but not over-cooked, as the oven will only re-heat them. Melt the butter in a saucepan, and add the flour to make a roux or thickening paste. Stirring constantly, add the stock and seasoning. Stir until smooth and slightly thickened. Add the chicken and vegetables, and simmer for 2 to 3 minutes.

Place the mixture into one large, or four individual, casserole dishes. Spoon the biscuit batter over the top of the casserole. You may leave the edges open, or bring the crust to the edges, whichever you prefer.

Bake for 15 to 20 minutes until the crust is golden-brown.

Shepherd's Pie
Topped with Cheddar Mashed Potatoes

Tillamook Cheddar makes any dish better. Taste the difference in this traditional dish.

Serves 8

INGREDIENTS

2 pounds extra-lean ground beef

2 tablespoons vegetable oil

1 cup diced onion

1 large carrot, diced

1 teaspoon minced garlic

2 tablespoons Worcestershire sauce

3 tablespoons tomato paste

1 (14-ounce) can crushed tomatoes

1/4 teaspoon freshly ground black pepper

4 cups mashed potatoes

4 cups shredded Tillamook Sharp Cheddar cheese, divided

2 tablespoons freshly chopped parsley

PREPARATION

Preheat the oven to 375°F.

Heat the oil in a large skillet over medium-high heat. Sauté the onion and carrot until softened, about 8 to 10 minutes. Add the garlic, and cook for 3 minutes. Stir in the ground beef, and cook until browned. Add the Worcestershire, tomato paste, crushed tomatoes, and pepper, and cook about 10 minutes, or until the mixture thickens. Spoon into a 9 by 13-inch baking dish.

Combine the mashed potatoes with 1/2 of the cheese and the parsley in a medium bowl. Spread the potato mixture on top of the beef. Top with the remaining cheese. Place the pan on a baking sheet and bake for 25 minutes until bubbling.

Mariner Frank Hemingway holds a photo of the Morning Star II and a sample of the new packaging that first featured the Morning Star logo. The packaging was redesigned in 1966 in order to make it easier to identify genuine Tillamook cheese. 1966

Tillamook Bay Cheese Bake

This tasty dish can also be served as a brunch or breakfast item.

Serves 4 to 6

INGREDIENTS

1/2 pound fresh bay shrimp
4 cups grated Tillamook Monterey Jack cheese
4 cups grated Tillamook Medium Cheddar cheese
1/4 cup chopped green onion
6 eggs, separated
1 cup canned evaporated milk, undiluted (or half-and-half)
2 tablespoons all-purpose flour
1/2 teaspoon salt
1/2 teaspoon freshly ground black pepper
1/4 teaspoon basil
6 to 8 canned artichoke hearts, quartered
2 to 3 medium tomatoes, sliced

PREPARATION

Preheat the oven to 325°F.

Combine the cheese, shrimp, and green onions. Beat the egg whites until stiff. In another bowl, combine the egg yolks, milk, flour, salt, pepper, and basil. Fold the beaten egg white into the egg-yolk mixture. Fold in the cheese and shrimp mixture. Turn into a well-buttered oblong baking dish (12 by 8-inch) and arrange the artichoke quarters evenly over the casserole. Bake for 30 minutes. Remove from the oven and arrange the tomato slices, overlapping slightly, over the top of the casserole. Bake an additional 15 to 20 minutes, until set. Cool for a few minutes before cutting into squares and serving.

Submitted by Judy Hessel
Sunset Magazine Contest Winner

Hazelnut-Crusted Salmon
with Pesto Cheddar Sauce

The richness of the hazelnuts complements the savory salmon and pesto.

Serves 4

INGREDIENTS

4 (6-ounce) center-cut salmon fillets, skin removed
1 1/2 cups whipping cream
1 1/2 tablespoons chopped garlic
1/3 cup minced fresh basil, flat-leaf parsley, or combination
1 teaspoon freshly squeezed lemon juice
Salt
Freshly ground black pepper
1/2 cup all-purpose flour
2 large eggs, lightly beaten
1 1/2 cups coarsely ground hazelnuts
2 cups shredded Tillamook Vintage White Extra Sharp Cheddar cheese, divided
Additional sprigs of basil or parsley, to garnish

PREPARATION

Bring the cream and the garlic to a boil in a small saucepan. Reduce the heat and boil, uncovered, until it has reduced to 1 cup, about 10 to 15 minutes. Remove from heat and stir in the herbs. Cover, and let stand for 15 minutes.

Process the cream mixture in a blender until smooth. Return to a clean saucepan, stir in the lemon juice. Reserve while cooking the salmon.

Preheat the oven to 400°F. Cover a baking sheet with foil or parchment paper.

Rinse the salmon and pat dry. Sprinkle with salt and pepper. Dredge in the flour, dip in the egg, and roll in the hazelnuts to cover thoroughly. Place on a baking sheet, and bake until the salmon is just opaque, about 10 to 15 minutes.

Meanwhile, bring the cream mixture to boil. Reduce the heat to low and slowly add 1 1/2 cups of the cheese. Cook, stirring constantly, until the cheese melts, about 1 to 2 minutes. Remove from the heat and season with salt and pepper.

To serve, arrange the salmon on serving plates and spoon the sauce over the fillets. Sprinkle with the remaining cheese. Garnish with more herbs, if desired.

STANDING (l to r): Richard, Ryan, Pam (in front of Ryan), Hannah (in Pam's arms), Holly, Stephanie, Chris, Olivia, Todd

SITTING (l to r): Frieda, Hallie, Ethan, Dylan

Breakfast & Brunch

Richard and Pam Obrist
Fairview Acres Dairy Farm

"We've worked hard all these years to produce good-quality milk, and we will continue as long as we can."

In 1920, when Andreas and Katherine Theoni emigrated to Tillamook from Canton Bern, Switzerland, they knew that they would be making cheese in America, just as they did in their homeland. One of their prized possessions was a copper cheese-making pot. However, the item was quickly outgrown as the family became a part of the dairying community in Tillamook.

These days, three generations live on the farm— Andreas and Katherine's daughter Frieda, Frieda's son Richard, his wife Pam, and their three sons Ryan, Todd, and Chris. Richard is very involved in various committees, and stresses that the dairy farmer's voice is vital in the industry. He says, "I am proud to have all three of my sons working alongside me on the dairy."

Smoothies

Smoothies are a perfect (and easy!) way to start the day. Depending on the season, add other fruits or berries to any of these recipes to create your personal flair.

Banana Bavaria Smoothie

Serves 1

INGREDIENTS
1 cup cold milk
1 ripe banana, smashed
1 scoop Tillamook chocolate ice cream

PREPARATION
Place all the ingredients into a blender and blend until smooth. Top with scoop of ice cream, if desired.

Banana Fruit Shake

Serves 4

INGREDIENTS
2 cups Tillamook Vanilla Bean yogurt
2 cups cranberry juice
1 cup banana slices
1 cup coarsely chopped fresh or canned peaches
1 tablespoon honey
1/4 teaspoon cinnamon
2 ice cubes

PREPARATION
Place all the ingredients into a blender and blend until smooth.

Strawberry Fling Smoothie

Serves 1

INGREDIENTS
1 cup Tillamook Vanilla Bean yogurt
3/4 cup milk
1 (10-ounce) package frozen, sweetened strawberries

PREPARATION
Place all the ingredients into a blender and blend until smooth.

Peach Mellow Smoothie

Serves 1

INGREDIENTS
3 canned or fresh peach halves
1 banana
1 cup Tillamook Peach yogurt
3/4 cup milk
2 tablespoons wheat germ (optional)

PREPARATION
Place all the ingredients into a blender and blend until smooth.

Zefiro Frittata

Frittatas come in many variations, and this one is one of the best—just enough veggies and meat to satisfy any appetite.

Serves 6

INGREDIENTS

2 potatoes, peeled and diced
1 cup olive oil
12 eggs, beaten
4 ounces cooked ham or prosciutto, diced or julienne
1 1/2 cups cubed or grated Tillamook Monterey Jack cheese
1 tablespoon freshly chopped thyme or parsley
1 red bell pepper, seeded and diced
Salt
Freshly ground black pepper

PREPARATION

Cook the potatoes in the olive oil in a nonstick skillet until just cooked. Be careful not to let the potatoes brown.

Drain the oil off the potatoes, and save the excess for future use. Add the potatoes to the beaten eggs. Add the remaining ingredients. Pour the mixture back into the hot skillet. Turn the flame down to medium low, and cook until the eggs are set.

Using a large plate, invert the frittata and slide it back into the skillet. Continue cooking until done. Slide out onto a large plate and cut into wedges. Serve hot or cold.

Created by Chef Christopher Israel
Portland, Oregon

Cheese & Egg Tartlets

Simple but delicious and filling!

Serves 4

INGREDIENTS

1 (10-ounce) tube refrigerated
buttermilk biscuits

1 (8-ounce) package brown-and-serve
sausage links, cooked

2 eggs

1/2 cup shredded Tillamook Medium
Cheddar cheese

3 tablespoons chopped green onions

PREPARATION

Preheat the oven to 400°F.

Roll out each biscuit into a 5-inch circle. Place each circle into an ungreased muffin cup. Cut the cooked sausage into fourths. Divide the sausages among the cups.

Combine the eggs, cheese, and onions in a small bowl. Spoon about 1 1/2 tablespoons of the mixture into each cup. Bake for 10 to 12 minutes, or until browned. Serve immediately.

Submitted by the Oregon Dairy
Farmers Association

1923 ad for Tillamook Cheese featuring a five cheese omelet recipe.

Eggs Florentine

This decadent breakfast is perfect paired with toasted English muffins.

Serves 4

INGREDIENTS
4 cups freshly chopped spinach,
  cooked, drained
4 eggs
Salt
Freshly ground black pepper
3/4 cups bread crumbs
2 tablespoons Tillamook butter, melted
1 cup evaporated milk
1/2 cup shredded Tillamook Vintage
  White Extra Sharp Cheddar cheese
1 tablespoon grated white onion

PREPARATION
Preheat the oven to 350°F.

Spread the spinach in the bottom of a shallow baking dish. With a fork, form 4 nests in the spinach, and drop an egg into each nest. Season the eggs to taste with salt and pepper.

Toss the bread crumbs with the melted butter. Reserve.

Meanwhile, heat the milk and cheese over a double boiler, stirring constantly, until the cheese melts. Stir in the onion. Pour the cheese sauce over the eggs and spinach. Sprinkle with the buttered breadcrumbs. Bake for 25 minutes.

Morning Cheddar Polenta
with Praline Bacon

Sweet, spicy, crispy, crunchy, and creamy. An elegant way to start your day.

Serves 8

INGREDIENTS
16 slices bacon
6 tablespoons brown sugar
1 tablespoon chili powder
3/4 teaspoon coarsely ground black
  pepper
3/4 cup coarsely chopped pecans
6 cups water
1 1/2 cups coarse cornmeal (polenta)
1 teaspoon salt
2 tablespoons Tillamook butter
1 (8-ounce) package (2 cups) shredded
  Tillamook Sharp Cheddar cheese,
  divided

PREPARATION
Preheat the oven to 375°F.

To prepare the bacon, combine the brown sugar, chili powder, pepper, and pecans in a small bowl. Place the bacon slices on a foil-lined baking sheet and bake for about 12 minutes, or until they are just a little more than half cooked. Drain the bacon grease from the pan and place on paper towels to drain. Turn the bacon slices over and place back on pan, and sprinkle with the pecan-sugar mixture. Continue to bake for 10 to 12 minutes, or until the topping is well-browned and the bacon is crisp.

To prepare the polenta, bring the water to a boil in a medium saucepan. Whisk in the cornmeal and salt. Reduce the heat to low, stirring occasionally. Cook the polenta until it is thickened, about 30 minutes. Whisk in the butter and 1 cup of the cheese. Serve hot, or see Chef's Note for instructions on preparing a day ahead.

Divide the polenta among 8 plates, top with the remaining cheese, and garnish each with 2 strips of the praline bacon.

CHEF'S NOTE
To make the polenta a day ahead: While the polenta is still hot, rinse and drain a 9 by 13-inch baking pan. Spread the polenta in the pan and let cool. Cover and refrigerate until ready to use.

TO REHEAT
Remove the cover, and bake at 350°F until heated through, about 20 minutes. Top with the remaining cup of cheese and return to the oven until the cheese is melted. Cut into 8 pieces and serve with the praline bacon.

Sun-Dried Tomato & Cheddar Cheese Soufflé

Better than scrambled eggs, and almost just as easy!

Serves 2

INGREDIENTS
1/4 cup Tillamook butter
1/2 cup all-purpose flour
3 tablespoons finely chopped, oil-
    packed, sun-dried tomatoes
1 cup milk, scalded
Pinch of salt
Pinch of nutmeg
Pinch of freshly ground black pepper
1/2 cup grated Tillamook Medium
    Cheddar cheese
3 egg yolks
3 egg whites, beaten

PREPARATION
Preheat the oven to 400°F.

Combine the butter, flour, and tomatoes in a large saucepan.

Season the milk with the salt, pepper, and nutmeg. Add the seasoned milk to the tomato mixture, and bring to a boil over medium-high heat. Remove from the heat, and add the cheese, egg yolks, and egg whites, and mix together. Pour the mixture into greased and floured soufflé cups. Bake for 10 minutes.

Created by Mark Hansberry
Columbia Gorge Hotel
Hood River, Oregon

What Are Curds and Whey?

"Little Miss Muffet sat on her tuffet eating her curds and whey..." The cheesemaking process begins when the solids in milk begin to separate from the whey. The more whey a cheesemaker drains from the curds the drier the cheese will be. Cottage cheese is an example of a cheese that still contains a good deal of whey. Parmesan cheese, on the other hand, contains very little whey. Miss Muffet was likely eating a watery form of cottage cheese.

Breakfast Sandwich

with Asparagus, Ham & Eggs

Start your day off right with this gourmet sandwich.

Makes 4 sandwiches

INGREDIENTS

16 asparagus spears, washed, trimmed
1/2 teaspoon olive oil
Salt
Freshly ground black pepper
2 teaspoons Tillamook butter
6 eggs, lightly beaten
4 (1/2-inch-thick) slices walnut bread
4 ounces Black Forest ham, at room temperature
4 ounces Tillamook Vintage White Medium Cheddar cheese, cut into 4 slices

PREPARATION

Preheat the oven to 475°F.

Place the asparagus on a baking sheet and drizzle with the oil. Season to taste with salt and pepper. Bake for 5 to 8 minutes, until the asparagus is tender. Remove the asparagus from the pan. Melt the butter in a medium skillet over medium-low heat. Pour in the eggs and cook, stirring gently, until the eggs are done. Remove from the heat. Season to taste with salt and pepper.

Preheat the broiler.

To assemble, lightly toast the bread and place on a baking pan. Arrange equal portions of ham, asparagus, and eggs on each slice. Top with the cheese slices. Place the sandwiches under the broiler for about 1 minute, or until cheese melts. Serve immediately.

White Cheddar, Sage & Bacon Biscuits

A breakfast favorite, with the delicious flavors of bacon and sharp cheddar.

Makes approximately 9 biscuits

INGREDIENTS
2 cups all-purpose flour
2 teaspoons baking powder
2 teaspoons sugar
3/4 teaspoon baking soda
1/2 teaspoon salt
2 tablespoons finely chopped fresh
   sage leaves
5 tablespoons cold Tillamook unsalted
   butter, cut into 1/2-inch pieces
5 bacon slices, cooked crisp, chopped
3/4 cup grated, Tillamook Vintage
   White Extra Sharp Cheddar cheese
3/4 cup buttermilk

PREPARATION
Place the rack in the middle of the oven and preheat to 425°F.

Sift together the flour, baking powder, sugar, baking soda, and salt and place in a large bowl. Stir in the sage and, using your fingertips, blend in the butter until the mixture is crumbly and resembles coarse meal.

Stir in the bacon and the cheese. Add the buttermilk, and stir just until the mixture begins to form a dough. Gather the dough into a ball, and on a lightly floured surface, knead gently 8 times.

Pat out the dough into a round, 3/4-inch thick. Cut the dough with a biscuit cutter, and place 1-inch apart on a baking sheet. Bake the biscuits for 15 minutes, or until golden-brown.

Skillet Breakfast

This is a great way to use leftover roast.

Serves 4

INGREDIENTS
4 to 5 small potatoes, sliced
2 teaspoons vegetable oil
1/2 onion, chopped
1/4 green bell pepper, chopped
2 cups cooked, cubed roast beef
6 to 7 eggs, scrambled
1 cup grated Tillamook Medium
  Cheddar cheese
Salsa (recipe follows)

SALSA
1/4 green bell pepper, finely chopped
1 small onion, finely chopped
1 to 2 cloves garlic, finely chopped
1/4 cup finely chopped cilantro
1 to 2 jalapeño peppers (more if
  needed), finely chopped
4 to 5 tomatoes, finely chopped
Pinch of salt
Pinch of freshly ground black pepper
Dash of freshly squeezed lemon juice

PREPARING THE SALSA
Combine all the ingredients in a medium bowl and toss gently to combine.

PREPARATION
Brown the sliced potatoes in the oil in a large skillet. Add the onion, pepper, and roast beef, and cook until the potatoes are browned and fork-tender. Add the eggs and cheese, and cook until the eggs are firm. Top with fresh salsa, and serve.

Submitted by Ben Stearns
KJSN Radio Recipe Contest

Why is Milk White?

Milk is always white since it contains casein, a white, calcium-rich protein, and white cream, although, low or non-fat milk may look less white due to less cream in the milk. And if you want to get scientific about it, white reflects light. Since the molecules that make up casein and cream are white and reflecting the light back to your eyes, milk appears to be very white.

Tillamook Breakfast Crêpe

Like enchiladas for breakfast? Kick-start your day with spice and flavor!

Serves 2 to 3

INGREDIENTS
3 (10-inch) egg crêpes, or flour tortillas
Green Chili Salsa (recipe follows)
1/4 cup Tillamook Medium Cheddar
   cheese

GREEN CHILI SALSA
3 fresh green chilis, roasted, seeded,
   stemmed, pitted (canned chilis may
   be substituted)
2 cloves garlic, finely chopped
1 tablespoon olive oil
1 cup chicken broth

EGG FILLING
6 eggs
2 tablespoons Tillamook butter
1 tomato, peeled, seeded, diced
3 green chilis, chopped

PREPARING THE GREEN CHILI SALSA
Chop the chilis until they are the consistency of relish. Sauté the garlic in the olive oil until it is golden. Add the chili and sauté until tender. Add the broth, and bring to a boil. Reduce the heat and simmer for 15 minutes, until thick and chunky. Remove from the heat and allow to cool to room temperature.

PREPARING THE EGG FILLING
Scramble the eggs in the butter in a medium skillet. As they begin to set, stir in the diced tomatoes and green chilis. When set thoroughly, but still tender, remove from the heat. Salt and pepper lightly.

ASSEMBLY
Warm the crêpes in the oven. Remove and place the egg filling across the crêpes. Add just enough salsa to moisten. Roll up, seam-side down. Top with the salsa and cheese. Place in the oven to melt the cheese.

Pacific Salmon Gravlax Benedict

This takes a little extra time, but it's an elegant treat.

Serves 4 to 6

SALMON GRAVLAX

1 (16-ounce) salmon fillet, preferable skin on
1/4 cup plus 2 tablespoons salt
1/4 cup plus 2 tablespoons sugar
2 whole bay leaves, crushed
1 tablespoon cracked fennel seeds
1/2 teaspoon cracked black peppercorns
2 ounces chopped fennel fronds
1 ounce gin

CHEDDAR SCALLION BISCUITS

1/2 cup medium-ground cornmeal
2 cups all-purpose flour
3 tablespoons baking powder
1 teaspoon baking soda
1/4 teaspoon cayenne pepper
1 1/2 teaspoons salt
3 ounces cold unsalted butter
2 cups shredded Tillamook Garlic White Cheddar cheese
5 scallions, chopped
1 3/4 cups buttermilk
Melted butter, to finish

BROWN BUTTER HOLLANDAISE

8 ounces butter
1 teaspoon water
3 egg yolks
1/4 teaspoon kosher salt
2 1/2 tablespoons freshly squeezed lemon juice

PREPARING THE SALMON GRAVLAX

Make sure that the salmon has been scaled and the pin bones removed. Combine the salt, sugar, bay leaves, fennel seeds, peppercorns, fennel fronds, and gin and mix well. Rub the salt mixture into the flesh side of the fillet, coating it thoroughly. Wrap the fish tightly in plastic wrap. Place the seasoned, wrapped fish in a nonreactive dish. Place a 1-pound weight on top and allow to cure, refrigerated, for 36 to 48 hours. Turn the fish every 12 hours. Fish should be firm, but not hard. Rinse off the cure and pat dry. Slice paper-thin.

PREPARING THE CHEDDAR SCALLION BISCUITS

Preheat the oven to 400°F.

Combine the cornmeal, flour, baking powder, baking soda, cayenne and salt in a food processor. Add the butter and pulse until the mixture is crumbly. Place the mixture in a mixing bowl. Add the cheese and scallions. Slowly mix in the buttermilk until it is well-combined and the dough is tacky. Place 2 heaping tablespoons of the mixture onto a cookie sheet, leaving 2 inches between the biscuits. Bake for 15 minutes. Brush with melted butter. Bake for 5 more minutes, or until golden-brown.

PREPARING THE BROWN BUTTER HOLLANDAISE

Place the butter in a medium-sized saucepan over medium-high heat. Once the solids have separated whisk until they just start to brown. Remove from heat and allow to cool slightly. Pour several cups of water into a medium-sized saucepan, bring it to a boil and turn off the heat. Place the egg yolks and 1 teaspoon of water into a medium mixing bowl and whisk until the mixture lightens in color. Place the egg yolk and water mixture over the hot water bath and continue whisking until a clear line is drawn in the yolk mixture when the whisk passes through it. Gradually add the butter, continually whisking until all the butter has been mixed in and the sauce is smooth. Season with salt and lemon juice. Serve immediately or store warm.

Dustin Clark, Chef
Wildwood Restaurant
Portland, OR

Crabmelt
with Tillamook Cheddar Cheese

Enjoy the layers of rich, sweet crab, deliciously creamy Cheddar cheese, and juicy tomato. For a beautiful presentation, julienne-cut the slices of cheese and create a criss-cross pattern.

Serves 6

INGREDIENTS
12 ounces Dungeness Crab meat
2 English muffins
2 tablespoons mayonnaise
4 slices large tomato
8 slices Tillamook Cheddar cheese
4 poached or fried eggs (optional)
4 slices Roma tomato

PREPARATION
Preheat the broiler.

Split and toast the English muffins.

Spread the mayonnaise on each muffin. Place a slice of tomato and a slice of cheese on top. Place in a broiler and melt the cheese. If you are adding eggs, place one on each prepared muffin half. Divide the crab equally among each half and place another slice of cheese on top. Return to the broiler and melt the cheese over the crab.

When melted to the desired amount, top with the Roma tomato and serve.

CHEF'S NOTE
Crab can be heated before putting on the muffin, or used cold.

Chef Profile : Billy Hahn

"We use Tillamook Cheese at Jake's Famous Crawfish Restaurant because it is premium-quality cheese. And it's local...which is one of McCormick & Schmick's Restaurant Group's goals in all of their restaurants. In fact, we have always used Tillamook Cheddar cheese on our cheeseburgers," says Executive Chef Billy Hahn. "My favorite Tillamook Cheese is the Vintage White Extra Sharp Smoked Cheddar. When I first moved to Portland and discovered Tillamook Cheese, I was impressed with its flavor and quality. Coming from Michigan, which is so close to Wisconsin, I certainly knew good cheese! So, when I discovered this local cheese, I wanted to use it to reflect the quality of local craftsman, as well as to support their efforts."

Billy Hahn has been with McCormick & Schmick's Restaurant Group since 1981, and helped open two McCormick & Schmick's restaurants—the Fish House and Bar in Beaverton and the Harborside at the Marina on the Willamette River. With no formal training, but years of apprenticeship under talented chefs and restaurateurs, Billy has spent over thirty years in kitchens from his early years in Lansing, Michigan to his current post as executive chef within McCormick & Schmick's. His love of food and commitment to the best in cuisine is evident in the menus that he has developed over the years.

BACK (l to r):
Rob, John, Leith

FRONT (l to r):
Bill Rock, Amy,
Pat Rock

NOT PICTURED:
Will

Dessert

Amy and Robert Seymour
Seymour Dairy, Inc.

"I am proud to be a fourth-generation dairy farmer farming the land that has been in the family for over 100 years."

The original Rock/Seymour Dairy was established in Oretown, Oregon, in the 1890s by Samuel Hardy Rock, an English emigrant from Devon. The cows were milked by hand and the milk shipped by horse and cart. The farm was expanded in 1960 when Bill Rock, grandson of Samuel, purchased an additional seventy acres in nearby Cloverdale. Two more expansions followed in 1988 and 2000.

The Seymours continue the family tradition of dairy farming in beautiful Tillamook County. They are deeply appreciative of their ancestors and the hard work they put into making the farm what it is today. Amy Seymour, great-granddaughter of Samuel Hardy Rock, says "I want the farm to stay in the family for another 100 years!"

Hazelnut Praline Meringue Beehives
with Caramel Butter Pecan Ice Cream

"This rich, intense, multidimensional combination of flavors plays tricks with your tongue, satisfying the senses and leaving a lasting impression on the taste buds. This recipe uses only the finest Tillamook products to make a masterpiece dessert."
—Kristin Backman

Serves 4 to 6

HAZELNUT PRALINES
1 cup brown sugar
1 cup granulated sugar
3/4 cup whole milk
Pinch of salt
2 tablespoons Tillamook butter
1 teaspoon vanilla
1 cup toasted chopped hazelnuts

CARAMEL SAUCE
3 tablespoons Tillamook butter
1/2 cup whole milk
1 cup brown sugar
1 teaspoon vanilla

BEEHIVES
3/4 cup vanilla wafer cookie crumbs
1/4 cup granulated sugar
1 cup of prepared Hazelnut Pralines
   (recipe follows)
1/4 cup Tillamook butter
Tillamook Caramel Butter Pecan Ice
   Cream

MERINGUE
4 egg whites
1/2 cup granulated sugar

PRALINES

Combine the sugars, milk, and a pinch of salt in a saucepan. Stir constantly until the mixture reaches a rapid boil on medium-high heat. Allow to boil without stirring until it reaches 235°F. Remove from the heat. Stir in the butter, vanilla, and hazelnuts and continue stirring until the mixture begins to thicken. Spread out onto a buttered baking sheet. Allow to cool completely, then crumble into dime-sized pieces.

CARAMEL SAUCE

Combine the butter, milk, brown sugar, and vanilla in a saucepan. Bring to a boil, stirring constantly on medium-high heat. Allow to boil, without stirring, for about 5 minutes. Remove the sauce from the heat and cool to room temperature.

BEEHIVES

Mix together the cookie crumbs, sugar, Hazelnut Pralines, and butter. Press the mixture into 1-cup buttered round molds, about 1-centimeter thick. Fill the molds with the softened ice cream and transfer the molds to the freezer for 20 minutes, or until they have hardened. While the molds are freezing, prepare the meringue.

MERINGUE

Combine the egg whites and sugar, and beat on high until stiff peaks form. Spoon the meringue into a frosting pouch with a 1/4-inch circular opening tip. Remove the molds from the freezer and invert the mold onto an individual serving plate. Carefully cover the crumb crust with the meringue, starting at the bottom, circling around the base, and working your way up, creating a beehive appearance.

Drizzle the Meringue Beehive with the Caramel Sauce and the Hazelnut Pralines. Serve immediately.

Submitted by Elizabeth Guise
Tillamook Recipe Contest, Grand Prize Winner, 2001
Cook Off Location: Seattle, WA

Cheddar Apple Dandy

Cheddar and apples is the perfect combination. Add sugar and cinnamon and you have a classic dessert.

Serves 4 to 6

FILLING
6 cups sliced, peeled apples
1/4 cup sugar
2 tablespoons all-purpose flour
1 cup shredded Tillamook Sharp
   Cheddar cheese

TOPPING
3/4 cup all-purpose flour
1/4 cup sugar
1/2 teaspoon cinnamon
1/4 teaspoon salt
1/2 cup butter
1/2 cup shredded Tillamook Sharp
   Cheddar cheese

PREPARATION
Preheat the oven to 375°F.

PREPARING THE FILLING
Combine the apples, sugar, flour and the cheese. Place in a greased 8-inch square pan.

PREPARING THE TOPPING
Combine the flour, sugar, cinnamon, and salt. Cut in the butter until the mixture resembles coarse crumbs, and sprinkle over the apple mixture. Bake for 30 to 45 minutes. Top with the cheese, and return to the oven until cheese melts.

Facts about Cheddar:

Almost 90% of all cheese sold in the United States is classified as a Cheddar type cheese.

Cheddar cheese is named for the village of Cheddar in Somerset, England where it was first made sometime during the sixteenth century.

Cheddar cheese was introduced to Tillamook County when Peter McIntosh, a Canadian cheesemaker, was hired at a local creamery in 1893. He is credited with originating Tillamook's cheddar cheese recipe.

Tillamook Dessert Pears

This elegant dessert is easier than it looks and will tantalize the taste buds. A perfect ending to any meal!

Serves 4

FILLING

2 fresh Bartlett pears, halved, cored, and dipped in lemon juice
6 tablespoons Grand Marnier® liqueur
1 teaspoon Tillamook butter
1 tablespoon heavy cream
1 teaspoon sugar
1/2 cup shredded Tillamook Sharp Cheddar cheese
1/2 cup shredded Tillamook Monterey Jack (or Pepper Jack if you like it spicy)

PREPARATION

Preheat the broiler.

Melt the butter in a saucepan over medium-high heat. Add the liqueur, and bring to a low boil. Add the heavy cream and sugar, blending with a wire whip. Stir constantly until the mixture begins to thicken and caramelize. Remove from the heat. Spoon the mixture over the pears and top with the cheeses. Broil the pears until the cheese is bubbly.

Serve immediately.

My Mother's Comfort Pie

You can't go wrong with a home-baked apple pie. The cheddar in the crust and the filling makes it a family favorite.

Serves 4 to 6

CRUST
2 cups all-purpose flour
1/2 teaspoon salt
2/3 cup shortening
1/2 cup grated Tillamook Special
    Reserve Extra Sharp Cheddar cheese
5 tablespoons ice water

FILLING
5 to 6 firm, tart apples, peeled, cored,
    and sliced
2 tablespoons freshly squeezed lemon
    juice
1/2 cup sugar
1/4 cup flour
1 teaspoon cinnamon
1/4 teaspoon nutmeg
1/2 cup grated Tillamook Special
    Reserve Extra Sharp Cheddar cheese

PREPARATION
Preheat the oven to 425°F.

Place the flour and salt into a large bowl. Cut in the shortening and cheese until the mixture becomes crumbly and resembles coarse meal. Slowly add the water, while stirring, until the crumbled mixture begins to hold together and just until you can form the dough into a ball. Be careful not to overwork the dough. Roll out half of the dough on a floured board. Place in a 9-inch pan. Roll out the remaining dough.

Mix all the filling ingredients together. Fill the crust with the filling, then place the second crust on top. Prick the top and seal the edges.

Bake for 15 minutes. Reduce the heat to 350°F, and continue baking for 45 more minutes. Remove from the oven and place on a wire rack.

May be served warm or cold…with more cheese if desired!

Submitted by Frances Benthin
Oregon State Fair Contest Winner

Cherry Almond Biscotti
with Blackberry Chutney

A stylish start to any special day.

Makes 6 dozen

CHERRY ALMOND BISCOTTI
2 cups all-purpose flour
1/4 cup whole-wheat flour
1 teaspoon baking powder
1/2 teaspoon kosher salt
1/2 teaspoon freshly ground black
  pepper
1 teaspoon finely chopped fresh
  rosemary
3 large eggs, at room temperature
3/4 cup sugar
1 1/2 cups almonds, coarsely chopped
1/2 cup dried cherries, coarsely
  chopped
1/4 cup golden raisins

BLACKBERRY CHUTNEY
3 cups blackberries (fresh or frozen)
1 1/2 cups sugar, divided
1/4 teaspoon ground cumin
1/4 teaspoon cardamom seeds
  (optional)
1/2 teaspoon red chili flakes
2 1/2 tablespoons olive oil
3/4 teaspoon mustard seeds
1/2 tablespoon minced ginger
1 tablespoon minced garlic
3/4 cup apple cider vinegar
1 medium apple (Granny Smith or other
  tart apple) peeled, cored, coarsely
  chopped
3 tablespoons dried currants or
  coarsely chopped raisins
1 (3-inch long) cinnamon stick

PREPARING THE BISCOTTI
Preheat the oven to 350°F.

Sift together the flours, baking powder, salt, and pepper in a small bowl. Stir in the rosemary, and set aside.

Beat the eggs and sugar in a mixing bowl on high about 5 minutes until the mixture is pale yellow and thickened. Add the flour mixture and stir just until incorporated. Gently fold in the nuts, cherries, and raisins.

Line a large baking sheet with parchment paper. Using damp hands, form the mixture into 2 (13 by 12-inch) loaves on the baking sheet.

Bake for 20 to 25 minutes, until pale golden. Remove from the oven and allow to cool completely. Reduce the heat to 300°F. Transfer the loaves to a cutting board and cut into 1/4-inch slices. Place the slices on two large parchment-lined baking sheets, and bake for 8 minutes on each side until lightly golden. Transfer to racks to cool. Biscotti can be kept for a week in an airtight container at room temperature.

PREPARING THE CHUTNEY
Combine the blackberries and 1/2 cup of the sugar in a medium saucepan. Bring the mixture to a boil over medium heat. Reduce the heat, and simmer for 10 minutes, stirring occasionally. Pour the liquid through a mesh strainer held over a medium bowl to remove the seeds, pressing with the back of a wooden spoon to extract the liquid. Set aside.

Combine the cumin, cardamom, and red chili flakes in a small bowl, and set aside. Heat the oil over medium heat in a medium saucepan. Add the mustard seeds and cook until the seeds begin to pop, about 30 seconds. Stir in the ginger and garlic and cook for 1 minute. Add the reserved spice mixture and stir for a few seconds. Stir in the cider vinegar, apples, currants, cinnamon stick, the remaining cup of sugar, and the strained blackberry mixture.

Bring to a boil, reduce the heat and simmer for 50 minutes, stirring occasionally. The chutney will thicken as it cools. Transfer the chutney to a bowl to cool. Once it has cooled, cover, and refrigerate for one day to allow the flavors to meld. Discard the cinnamon stick before serving.

Chutney can be kept for one month, refrigerated in an airtight container.

Northwest Wine & Cheese Pairings

Tillamook Cheese recently brought together sixteen culinary experts, including our own head cheesemaker Dale Baumgartner, to taste Oregon and Washington cheese and wines. The result is one of the most robust pairing lists ever developed using Northwest wines and cheeses.

We hope this guide helps you get started, but we encourage you to explore and find your own favorite pairings.

Tillamook Cheese & Sparkling and White Wine Pairings

Sparkling Wine
Concentrated fruit aromas and flavors, including a blend of pear, apple and lemon-citrus.

Camembert
Camembert has a creamy, yellow flesh that is encased in a speckled, floury, moldy-looking crust. A perfectly ripe Camembert possesses a fruity, slightly tangy fragrance.

Chaource
This classic French soft-ripened cheese is made from cow's milk and is a double crème. The taste of Chaource has hints of mushrooms and a creamy, smooth finish.

Fontina
Italian-style Brindisi Fontina has a warm, golden glow and complex flavor, which develops over time from the lightly salted, shelf-aged hard rind, characteristic of the semi-soft cheese. Fontina lands sharply on the palate and mellows immediately.

Viognier
Sweet aromas of orange blossoms, honeysuckle, star fruit, melon and mango.

Tillamook Vintage White Extra Sharp Cheddar
This Cheddar is naturally aged for over two years, which allows it to develop an award-winning extra-sharp, bold, mature flavor and smooth, yet slightly crumbly, texture.

Chaource
This classic French soft-ripened cheese is made from cow's milk and is a double crème. The taste of Chaource has hints of mushrooms and a creamy, smooth finish.

Sauvignon Blanc
Aromas of ripe pear and honeysuckle lead to refreshing grapefruit flavors.

Tillamook Vintage White Extra Sharp Cheddar
This Cheddar is naturally aged for over two years, which allows it to develop an award-winning extra-sharp, bold, mature flavor and smooth, yet slightly crumbly, texture.

Herb de Provence
A semi-pressed, washed rind cheese, with a delicate nutty flavor. A combination of rosemary and sage with a finish of lavender.

Fontina
Italian-style Brindisi Fontina has a warm, golden glow and complex flavor, which develops over time from the lightly salted, shelf-aged hard rind, characteristic of the semi-soft cheese. Fontina lands sharply on the palate and mellows immediately.

Pinot Gris
Varietal expression with beautiful white flowers, such as honeysuckle, hinting of springtime freshness, while lending notes of crispness with citrus and grapefruit.

Tillamook Medium Cheddar
Naturally aged for over sixty days to develop its rich, creamy, smooth flavor.

Fontina
Italian-style Brindisi Fontina has a warm, golden glow and complex flavor, which develops over time from the lightly salted, shelf-aged hard rind, characteristic of the semi-soft cheese. Fontina lands sharply on the palate and mellows immediately.

Camembert

Camembert has a creamy, yellow flesh that is encased in a speckled, floury, moldy-looking crust. A perfectly ripe Camembert possesses a fruity, slightly tangy fragrance.

Chardonnay

Aromas are a high-toned honeysuckle blossom, citrus flower and star fruit mix with complex spices of vanilla and white pepper.

Tillamook Smoked Black Pepper White Cheddar
A burst of smoky, black-pepper flavor combined with the irresistible taste of aged creamy white Cheddar.

Tillamook Vintage White Extra Sharp Cheddar
This Cheddar is naturally aged for over two years, which allows it to develop an award-winning extra-sharp, bold, mature flavor and smooth, yet slightly crumbly, texture.

Blue
A semi-soft textured cheese characterized by blue veins of mold and a very strong aroma. Maytag (Iowa, US), Stilton (UK), Roquefort (France) and Gorgonzola (Italy) are all types of blue cheese.

Riesling

Delivers classic mineral and slate notes and lively, crisp acidity with juicy white peach aromas and flavors.

Tillamook Smoked Cheddar
This smoked medium Cheddar is aged sixty days and infused with natural hardwood smoke to produce its distinctive flavor.

Tillamook Vintage White Extra Sharp Cheddar
This Cheddar is naturally aged for over two years, which allows it to develop an award-winning extra-sharp, bold, mature flavor and smooth, yet slightly crumbly, texture.

Blue
A semi-soft textured cheese characterized by blue veins of mold and a very strong aroma. Maytag (Iowa, US), Stilton (UK), Roquefort (France) and Gorgonzola (Italy) are all types of blue cheese.

Tillamook Cheese & Red Wine Pairings

Whole Cluster Pinot Noir

Vibrant and explosive aromas of kiwi, blueberries, cherries and strawberries dominate with hints of sweet juice and warm spices. Flavors mirror aromas with blueberries, strawberries, and cherries dominating, complemented by juicy and spicy characters.

Tillamook Special Reserve Extra Sharp Cheddar
Naturally aged for over fifteen months to give it the most robust, most complex flavor of the yellow Cheddars.

Tillamook Vintage White Extra Sharp Cheddar
This Cheddar is naturally aged for over two years, which allows it to develop an award-winning extra-sharp, bold, mature flavor and smooth, yet slightly crumbly, texture.

Blue
A semi-soft textured cheese characterized by blue veins of mold and a very strong aroma. Maytag (Iowa, US), Stilton (UK), Roquefort (France) and Gorgonzola (Italy) are all types of blue cheese.

Pinot Noir

Vibrant aromas of cherries, spices, chocolate, rose petals, and vanilla. Initial silky impression with spicy flavors of nutmeg and barrel toast with ripe flavors of currants, cherries and mineral overtones.

Tillamook Vintage White Extra Sharp Smoked Cheddar
Naturally aged for over two years and infused with natural hardwood smoke to produce its distinctive award-winning extra-sharp, bold, mature flavor and smooth, yet slightly crumbly, texture.

Tillamook Vintage White Extra Sharp Cheddar
This Cheddar is naturally aged for over two years, which allows it to develop an award-winning extra-sharp, bold, mature flavor and smooth, yet slightly crumbly, texture.

Chaource
This classic French soft-ripened cheese is made from cow's milk and is a double crème. The taste of Chaource has hints of mushrooms and a creamy, smooth finish.

Cabernet Franc

Aromas of Anaheim peppers, white pepper, floral red and black fruits, cola and cedar spice.

Tillamook Smoked Black Pepper White Cheddar
A burst of smoky, black-pepper flavor combined with the irresistible taste of aged creamy white Cheddar.

Tillamook Vintage White Extra Sharp Smoked Cheddar
Naturally aged for over two years and infused with natural hardwood smoke to produce the distinctive award-winning extra-sharp, bold, mature flavor and smooth, yet slightly crumbly, texture.

Tillamook Pepper Jack
Blends the mellow essence of Monterey Jack with the spicy zing of jalapeño peppers to create a flavor that both comforts and invigorates.

Merlot

Rich and spicy, with aromas of nutmeg, clove and cinnamon, this wine shows ripe black plum, blackberry and dark flavors encased in a peppery, chocolate, black-cherry finish.

Tillamook Vintage White Extra Sharp Cheddar
This Cheddar is naturally aged for over two years, which allows it to develop an award-winning extra-sharp, bold, mature flavor and smooth, yet slightly crumbly, texture.

Gouda
Has a nutty and strong aromatic flavor. Textures range from semi-hard to soft, encapsulated by a distinctive natural rind.

Blue
A semi-soft textured cheese characterized by blue veins of mold and a very strong aroma. Maytag (Iowa, US), Stilton (UK), Roquefort (France) and Gorgonzola (Italy) are all types of blue cheese.

Syrah

This intense wine is layered with flavors of coffee and menthol, hinting at chocolate and a toastiness flowing delicately at the finish.

Tillamook Garlic White Cheddar
For the true garlic lovers! The distinctive flavor of roasted garlic is skillfully blended with the creaminess of naturally aged white Cheddar.

Blue
A semi-soft textured cheese characterized by blue veins of mold and a very strong aroma. Maytag (Iowa, US), Stilton (UK), Roquefort (France) and Gorgonzola (Italy) are all types of blue cheese.

Fontina
Italian-style Brindisi Fontina has a warm, golden glow and complex flavor, which develops over time from the lightly salted, shelf-aged hard rind, characteristic of the semi-soft cheese. Fontina lands sharply on the palate and mellows immediately.

Tempranillo

Aromas of blackberries and blueberries, crushed fruit, spice, roasted nuts, and unimposing oak. Finishing with licorice, leather and caramel.

Tillamook Vintage White Extra Sharp Cheddar
This Cheddar is naturally aged for over two years, which allows it to develop an award-winning extra-sharp, bold, mature flavor and smooth, yet slightly crumbly, texture.

Tillamook Medium Cheddar
Naturally aged for over sixty days to develop its rich, creamy, smooth flavor.

Gouda
Has a nutty and strong aromatic flavor. Textures range from semi-hard to soft, encapsulated by a distinctively natural rind.

Cabernet Sauvignon

Aromas of dense, dark fruit flavors showcasing cassis, black cherry and cocoa with leather, tobacco and savory spice on a balanced toasty finish.

Chaource
This classic French soft-ripened cheese is made from cow's milk and is a double crème. The taste of Chaource has hints of mushrooms and a creamy, smooth finish.

Smoky Blue
A smoked version of the semi-soft textured cheese characterized by blue veins of mold and a very strong aroma. Maytag (Iowa, US), Stilton (UK), Roquefort (France) and Gorgonzola (Italy) are all types of blue cheese.

Camembert
Camembert has a creamy, yellow flesh that is encased in a speckled, floury, moldy-looking crust. A perfectly ripe Camembert possesses a fruity, slightly tangy fragrance.

Award-Winning Cheeses

1904   St. Louis World's Fair
Gold Medal for cheese awarded to Thomas Ballantine from Nehalem

1926   Pacific Slope Dairy Show
First Place for Cheddar cheese to Albert Schlappi

1928   Pacific Slope Dairy Show
Third Place for Cheddar cheese to Ed Schlappi

1937   Pacific International Livestock Expo
Silver Medal for Cheddar cheese to Ivan Knight

1940   Pacific International Livestock Expo
Silver Medal for fresh Cheddar cheese to Ivan Knight
Bronze Medal for aged Cheddar cheese to Ivan Knight

1941   Oregon Dairy Manufacturers Association
Gold Medal for Cheddar cheese to Ivan Knight

1941   Pacific International Livestock Expo
Bronze Medal for fresh Cheddar cheese to Ivan Knight

1942   Oregon Diary Manufacturers Association
Gold Medal for Cheddar cheese to Ivan Knight

1950   California State Fair
Gold Medal for cheese to Harold Sutton

1951   California State Fair
Gold Medal for cheese to Harold Sutton

1951   Tillamook County Fair
First Place for "fresh" cheese to Wilfred Lommen
Second Place for "fresh" cheese to Lloyd Seufert
Third Place for "fresh" cheese to R.B. Price
Fourth Place for "fresh" cheese to Gordon Long
Fifth Place for "fresh" cheese to Harold Sutton
First Place for aged cheese to R.B. Price
Second Place for aged cheese to Basil Tone
Third Place for aged cheese to Wilfred Lommen
Fourth Place for aged cheese to Norman Christensen
Fifth Place for aged cheese to C.A. Hutchens

1952   California State Fair
Gold Medal for cheese to Harold Sutton
Silver Medal for aged cheese to Harold Sutton

1954   California State Fair & Exposition
Gold Medal for aged cheese to Harold Sutton

1957   California State Fair & Exposition
2 Gold Medals for cheese

1958   California State Fair & Exposition
2 Gold Medals for cheese

1960   Oregon Dairy Industries
First Place for aged cheese to Harold Sutton
Second Place for aged cheese to James Gulstrom
First Place for medium aged cheese to Mert Loucks
Third Place for medium aged cheese to Fritz Baumgartner

1961   Oregon Dairy Industries
Third Place for aged Cheddar to Harold Sutton
First Place for medium Cheddar to Bud Etzwiler
Second Place for medium Cheddar to Mert Loucks
Third Place for medium Cheddar to Alfred Long

1961   Tillamook County Fair
First Place for aged Cheddar (96 points) to Mert Loucks
Second Place for aged Cheddar (95.5 points) to Jim Gulstrom
Third Place for aged Cheddar (95 points) to Wilfred Lommen
Fourth Place for aged Cheddar (94.5 points) to Gordon Hussey
Fifth Place for aged Cheddar (94 points) to John Powers
First Place for fresh Cheddar (96 points) to Bud Etzwiler
Second Place for fresh Cheddar (95.5 points) to Donley Lommen
Third Place for fresh Cheddar (95 points) to Harold Sutton
Fourth Place for fresh Cheddar (94.5 points) to Gordon Hussey
Fifth Place for fresh Cheddar (94 points) to Roy Gallino

1962   Tillamook County Fair
First Place for fresh cheese (95 points) to Bud Etzwiler
Second Place for fresh cheese (94.5 points) to Gunnard Pylkki
Third Place for fresh cheese (94 points) to Gordon Hussey
Fourth Place for fresh cheese (94 points) to Fritz Baumgartner
Fifth Place for fresh cheese (93.5 points) to Harold Sutton
First Place for aged cheese (95 points) to Donley Lommen
Second Place for aged cheese (94.5 points) to Bud Etzwiler
Third Place for aged cheese (94 points) to Gordon Hussey
Fourth Place for aged cheese (93.5 points) to Gunnard Pylkki
Fifth Place for aged cheese (93 points) to Lloyd Seufert

1965   Oregon Dairy Industries
First Place for aged Cheddar to Gordon Hussey
First Place for medium aged Cheddar to Lloyd Wright
Third Place for medium aged Cheddar to Jim Brunson
Third Place for aged Cheddar to Ed Yates
Honorable Mention for medium aged Cheddar to Lloyd Wright

1966   Oregon Dairy Industries
First Place for aged Cheddar to John Reich

1968   Oregon Dairy Industries
First Place for aged Cheddar to Fritz Baumgartner
Second Place for aged Cheddar to Ron Jones
Second Place for aged Cheddar to Lloyd Wright
Third Place for aged Cheddar to Mert Loucks
Third Place for aged Cheddar to Allen Waldron
First Place for medium aged Cheddar to Dean Daggett
Second Place for medium aged Cheddar to Fritz Baumgartner
Third Place for medium aged Cheddar to Mert Loucks
Fourth Place for medium aged Cheddar to Ed Yates
Fourth Place for medium aged Cheddar to Allen Waldron
Fourth Place for medium aged Cheddar to Lloyd Wright
Honorable Mention for medium aged Cheddar to Lloyd Wright

1971   Oregon Dairy Industries
First Place for aged Cheddar
First Place for medium aged Cheddar

1978   Oregon Dairy Industries
Gold Medal for Cheddar cheese
First Place for medium Cheddar cheese
Silver Medal for cheese to Jim Gulstrom
Silver Medal for cheese to Mert Loucks

1979   Oregon Dairy Industries
Silver Medal for Cheddar cheese to Ed Yates

1981   Oregon Dairy Industries
First Place for Cheddar cheese

1982   Oregon Dairy Industries
Gold Medal for Cheddar cheese
Silver Medal for Cheddar cheese

1983   Oregon Dairy Industries
First Place for Cheddar cheese

1986   Oregon Dairy Industries
First Place for Cheddar cheese

1986   Governor's Award for Corporate Excellence

1987   Oregon Dairy Industries
Gold Medal for medium Cheddar cheese

1988   Oregon Dairy Industries
Gold Medal for medium Cheddar cheese
Second Place for medium Cheddar cheese

1992   Oregon Dairy Industries
First Place for medium Cheddar cheese

1992   NMPF Cheese Contest
Second Place for aged Cheddar cheese
Second Place for medium Cheddar cheese

1993   NMPF Cheese Contest
Second Place for aged Cheddar cheese
Second Place for medium Cheddar cheese

1993   Oregon Dairy Industries
First Place for sharp Cheddar cheese

1994   NMPF Cheese Contest
First Place for medium Cheddar cheese
Second Place for unique or flavored cheese
President's Trophy for Most Outstanding Cheese

1994   Oregon Dairy Industries
First Place for medium Cheddar cheese

1995   Oregon Dairy Industries
Gold Medal for medium Cheddar cheese

1995   NMPF Cheese Contest
Second Place for medium Cheddar cheese

1996   NMPF Cheese Contest
First Place for medium Cheddar cheese
First Place for aged Cheddar cheese
Third Place for Pepper Jack in the Unique or Flavored category
Second Place for aged Cheddar cheese

1997   NMPF Cheese Contest
Second Place for Natural Cheese
Second Place for mild Cheddar cheese
Second Place for aged Cheddar
Second Place for unique or flavored cheese
Second Place for medium Cheddar cheese

1998   British Empire Cheese Show
First Place for Mature Cheddar cheese
Fourth Place for medium Cheddar

1998   Oregon Dairy Industries
Gold Medal for medium aged Cheddar cheese

1998   NMPF Cheese Contest
First Place for mild Cheddar cheese
Third Place for mild Cheddar cheese
First Place for medium Cheddar cheese
Second Place for medium Cheddar cheese
Second Place for aged Cheddar cheese
Third Place for aged Cheddar cheese
Second Place for Monterey Jack cheese
Third Place for Monterey Jack cheese
Second Place for Pepper Jack cheese
Fourth Place for Pepper Jack cheese
First Place for Monterey Jack reduced fat cheese
Third Place for Cheddar reduced fat cheese

1998   American Cheese Society
Second Place for Sharp White Cheddar cheese
Third Place for Pepper Jack cheese

1999   ODFA Presidential Award

1999   British Empire Cheese Show
Cheese Reporter Trophy, for being the highest-scoring cheese in the cheddar and specialty cheese categories made from a cheese-maker outside of Canada; presented to Dale Baumgartner

1999   NMPF Cheese Contest
First Place for medium Cheddar cheese
Second Place for Colby Jack cheese
Third Place for aged Cheddar cheese
Third Place for Colby Jack cheese
Third Place for mild Cheddar cheese
Third Place for Monterey Jack cheese

1999   Oregon Diary Industries
Gold Medal for medium aged Cheddar cheese

1999   United States Championship Cheese Contest
Second Place ribbon

2000   Fred Meyer Vendor of the Year Award

2000   Oregon Dairy Industries
First Place for medium aged Cheddar cheese

2000   World Championship Cheese Contest
Second Place for Colby Jack cheese (98.95 points)
Third Place for aged Cheddar cheese (97.25 points)

2000   NMPF Cheese Contest
First Place for aged white Cheddar cheese
Second Place for medium Cheddar cheese
Second Place for reduced fat Monterey Jack cheese
Third Place for medium Cheddar cheese

2001   American Cheese Society
First Place for Monterey Jack cheese, to Rob Burns
Second Place for Vintage White Cheddar, to Dale Baumgartner
Third Place for Special Reserve Cheddar cheese, to Rob Burns
Second Place for smoked Cheddar cheese, to Dale Baumgartner
Third Place for sharp Cheddar cheese

2001   Oregon Dairy Industry
First Place for medium aged Cheddar cheese
Gold Medal for medium aged Cheddar cheese

2001   NMPF Cheese Contest
Second Place for medium Cheddar cheese (98.65 points)
Second Place for aged Cheddar cheese (99.7 points)
First Place for aged Cheddar cheese (99.9 points)

2002   World Cheese Contest
Best of Class for flavored hard cheese (Jalapeño Jack) (99.8 points),
presented to Bob Walker

2002   NMPF Cheese Contest
First Place for aged Cheddar cheese
Second Place for mild Cheddar cheese
Third Place for aged Cheddar cheese
Third Place for medium Cheddar cheese

2002   Fred Meyer Vendor of the Year

2002   Idaho Milk Possessors Cheese Contest
Second Place for current Cheddar cheese, to Dale Baumgartner
Third Place for medium Cheddar cheese, to Dale Baumgartner
First Place for aged Cheddar cheese, to Dale Baumgartner
Second Place for aged Cheddar cheese, to Rob Burns

2003   Oregon Dairy Industries
Gold Medal for medium aged Cheddar

2003   NMPF Cheese Contest
Third Place for Pepper Jack in the Unique or Flavored Cheese
category, presented to Ed Sander

2003   Idaho Milk Processors Cheese Contest
Third Place for medium Cheddar cheese, presented to Bob Walker

2003   US Championship Cheese Contest
Second Place for Cheddar cheese, presented to Ed Sander
Fifth Place for Colby/Monterey Jack cheese, presented to Mike Jones
Ninth Place for Pepper Jack cheese in the Flavored/Hard category,
presented to Jim Reinhart

2004   Oregon Dairy Industries
Gold Medal for Cheddar cheese

2004   NMPF Cheese Contest
First Place for medium Cheddar cheese
Second Place for medium Cheddar cheese
First Place for Monterey Jack cheese
Third Place for Monterey Jack cheese
First Place for Pepper Jack cheese

2005   NMPF Cheese Contest
First Place for Monterey Jack cheese
Second Place for Monterey Jack cheese
First Place for Pepper Jack cheese
Second Place for Colby Jack cheese
Second Place for medium Cheddar cheese
Third Place for sharp Cheddar cheese
Second Place for mild Cheddar cheese
Third Place for mild Cheddar cheese
Fifth Place for Vintage White Medium Cheddar cheese

2006   Oregon Dairy Industries
First Place for medium Cheddar cheese

2006   NMPF Cheese Contest
First Place for Medium Vintage White Cheddar cheese
Best of Class for Medium Vintage White Cheddar cheese
First Place for mild Cheddar cheese
Second Place for Smoked Black Pepper Cheddar cheese
Second Place for medium Cheddar cheese
Third Place for aged Cheddar cheese

2007   Oregon Dairy Industries
First Place for medium Cheddar cheese

2007   American Cheese Society
Second Place for smoked Cheddar cheese
Second Place for Garlic Chili Pepper Cheddar cheese
Third Place for Smoked Black Pepper Cheddar cheese

2007   NMPF Cheese Contest
First Place for Vintage White Medium Cheddar cheese
Second Place for Medium Cheddar cheese
Third Place for Smoked Black Pepper Cheddar cheese

2008   Oregon Dairy Industries
First Place for medium Cheddar cheese

Credits

Grand Marnier® liqueur is a registered product of Marnier-Lapostolle, Inc.

Old Bay® Seasoning is a registered product of McCormick & Company, Inc.

Spice Hunter® granulated roasted garlic is a registered product of Spice Hunter, Inc.

Tabasco® Pepper Sauce is a registered product of McIlhenny Company.

Tillamook® Cheese is a registered product of Tillamook County Creamery Association (TCCA).

Tillamook® Butter is a registered product of Tillamook County Creamery Association (TCCA).

Tillamook® Yogurt is a registered product of Tillamook County Creamery Association (TCCA).

Tillamook® Ice Cream is a registered product of Tillamook County Creamery Association (TCCA).

Tillamook® Sour Cream is a registered product of Tillamook County Creamery Association (TCCA).

Tillamook Photography & Recipe Development

Catherine Healy (Flint Design Company), Recipe Direction and Creative Direction

Rachelle Fisher (Flint Design Company), Photo Art Direction

Carol Cooper Ladd and Lisa Lanxon, Recipe Development and Food Styling

Dennis Herron, Food Styling Assistant

Jane Zwinger, Recipe Development Assistant

Lori Emch, Recipe Development Assistant

Michael Shay (Polara Studios), Principle Food Photography

Jay Lawrence (Polara Studios), Photography Assistant

Recipe photos on pages: 6, 58, 104, 144, 148, 152, 156, 158, 166, 170, 176, 180

Rick Schafer, photographer

Teresa Schafer, food stylist

Supplemental photos on pages: xxviii, 38, 40, 68, 92, 94, 130, 154, 172, 174

Rick Schafer, photographer

Tillamook Photography Prop Credits

Appetizers

p. 6

Tillamook Cheese Nachos

Melina's Garden dinner plate, *courtesy Kitchen Kaboodle*

Salads, Soups, Sides

p. 58

Tortilla Chip Soup

Saleen Poly placemat, *courtesy Kitchen Kaboodle*

Basic napkin, Sapphire, *courtesy Kitchen Kaboodle*

Main Course

p. 148

Chicken Pot Pie with Tillamook Extra Sharp Cheddar and Green Onion Biscuit Crust

Deep-dish baker, *courtesy Le Creuset*

p. 144

Creamy Tillamook Cheese and Seafood Enchiladas

Luminarc Color Moods dinner plate, *courtesy Kitchen Kaboodle*

Basic napkin, Sapphire, *courtesy Kitchen Kaboodle*

p. 152

Hazelnut-Crusted Salmon with Pesto Cheddar Sauce

Aki Sienna salad plate, 7-inch, *courtesy Kitchen Kaboodle*

Breakfast/Brunch

p. 156

Smoothie Recipes

Gilbraltar 16-ounce cooler glasses, *courtesy Kitchen Kaboodle*

Melamine serving tray, 14 by 21-inch, *courtesy Kitchen Kaboodle*

p. 166

White Cheddar, Sage and Bacon Biscuits

Basic napkin, Sapphire, *courtesy Kitchen Kaboodle*

p. 158

Zefiro Frittata

All-Clad French skillet, 11-inch diameter, *courtesy Kitchen Kaboodle*

Dessert

p. 180

My Mother's Comfort Pie

Chantal deep-dish pie plate, *courtesy Kitchen Kaboodle*

p. 176

Hazelnut Praline Meringue Beehives with Caramel Butter Pecan Ice Cream

Sonoma salad plate, *courtesy Kitchen Kaboodle*

Concordance

Cheeses *(continued)*

Meats

Seafood

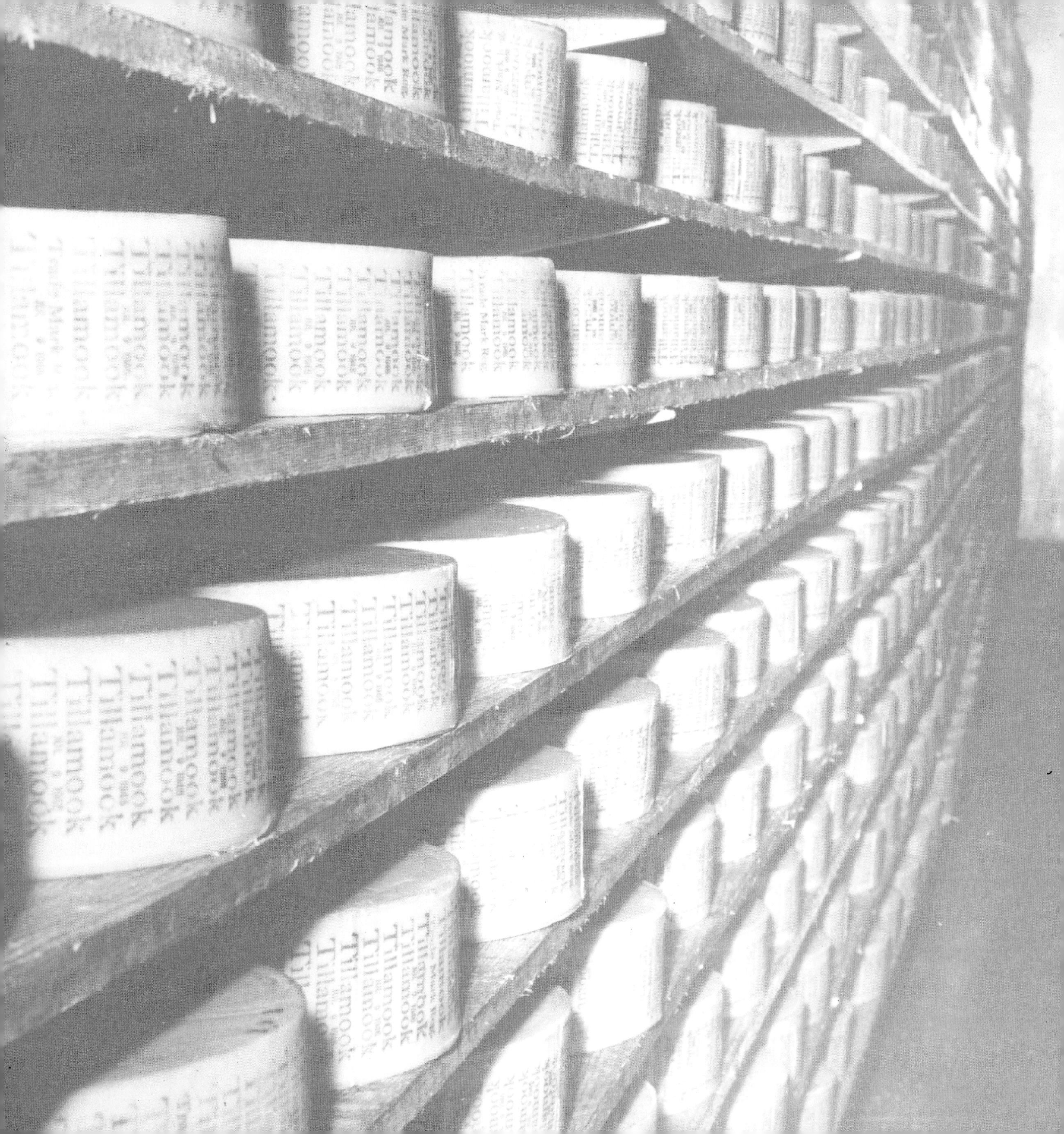
Tillamook